THEMATIC UNIT
Football

Written by Robert W. Smith

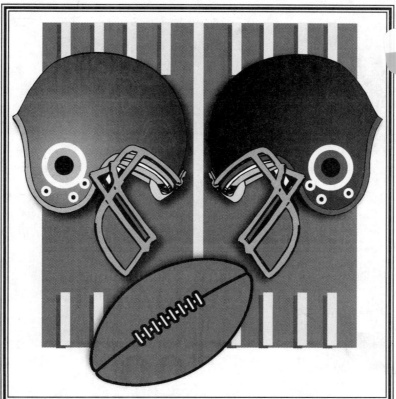

Teacher Created Materials, Inc.
6421 Industry Way
Westminster, CA 92683
www.teachercreated.com
©2003 Teacher Created Materials, Inc.
Made in U.S.A.
ISBN-0-7439-3105-X

Edited by
Karen Tam Froloff

Illustrated by
Bruce Hedges

Cover Art by
Denise Bauer

Table of Contents

Introduction

Football is an exciting whole-language unit that encompasses the history, rules, language, and strategy of football. These 80 pages are designed to introduce and immerse students into the game of football through math, history, language arts, and literature. The literature choices for this unit are certain to excite the interest of both boys and girls and to add to their knowledge of the game as well. A wide variety of teaching strategies is employed throughout the text to motivate and maintain the high interest of students. These include hands-on activities, cooperative learning groups, team-building activities, and full-class instruction. In addition, there are attractive units introducing Readers' Theater, poetry writing, creative expression, and physical education. Also included is a unit on learning the skills utilized in playing football. At the core of this literature-based theme book are two excellent literature selections: *Get That Girl Out of the Boys' Locker Room!* by Elaine Moore and *Catch That Pass!* by Matt Christopher.

This thematic unit includes the following:

❏ **literature selections**—summaries of the two books related to the topic of football

❏ **fine arts**—suggestions for activities in the visual arts

❏ **planning guidance**—sequenced lessons and activities to provide a natural flow of study, which increases understanding of the various components of football

❏ **bulletin boards**—suggestions and instructions for content-related bulletin boards

❏ **curriculum connections**—activities that interweave language arts, math, social studies, health, physical education, and art with football

❏ **culminating activities**—experiences that allow students to apply their learning

❏ **bibliography**—a list of resources and books, specifically related to football

❏ **answer key**—answers for activities in this unit

To keep this valuable resource intact so that it can be used year after year, you may wish to punch holes in the pages and store them in a three-ring binder.

Introduction *(cont.)*

Why a Balanced Approach?

The strength of a whole-language approach is that it involves children in using all modes of communication—reading, writing, listening, observing, illustrating, and doing. Communication skills are interconnected and integrated into lessons that emphasize the whole of language. Balancing this approach is our knowledge that every whole—including individual words—is composed of parts, and directed study of those parts can help a student to master the whole. Experience and research tell us that regular attention to phonics, other word-attack skills, and spelling develops reading mastery, thereby fulfilling the unity of the whole-language experience. The child is thus led to read, write, spell, speak, and listen confidently in response to a literature experience introduced by the teacher. In these ways, language skills grow rapidly, stimulated by direct practice, involvement, and interest in the topic at hand.

Why Thematic Planning?

One very useful tool for implementing a balanced language program is thematic planning. By choosing a theme with correlating literature selections for a unit of study, a teacher can plan activities throughout the day that lead to a cohesive, in-depth study of the topic. Students will be practicing and applying their skills in meaningful contexts. Consequently, they will tend to learn and retain more. Both teachers and students will be freed from a day that is broken into unrelated segments of isolated drill and practice.

Why Cooperative Learning?

Besides academic skills and content, students need to learn social skills. This area of development cannot be taken for granted. Students must learn to work cooperatively in groups in order to function well in modern society. Group activities should be a regular part of school life, and teachers should consciously include social objectives as well as academic objectives in their planning. For example, a group working together to solve a problem may need to select a leader. Teachers should make clear to the students the qualities of good leader-follower group interaction just as they would state and monitor the academic goals of the project.

Four Basic Components of Cooperative Learning

1. *In cooperative learning, all group members need to work together to accomplish the task.*

2. *Cooperative learning groups should be heterogeneous.*

3. *Cooperative learning activities need to be designed so that each student contributes to the group, and individual group members can be assessed on their performance.*

4. *Cooperative learning teams need to know the social as well as the academic objectives of a lesson.*

Get That Girl Out of the Boys' Locker Room!

by Elaine Moore

Summary

Michelle Dupree may be the smallest seventh grade girl in Jefferson Junior High, but she is a superb athlete. In the sixth grade, she and her two best friends, Sandy and Skye, had starred on their school's coed basketball team. After watching Michelle casually boot a football through the uprights, three boys from her basketball team and her older brother, Brian, convince Michelle to try out for the boys' football team, which is in desperate need of a capable kicker.

But there is one problem—the football coach would never tolerate a girl on the team. So Michelle and her friends arrange a variety of subterfuges to conceal her identity. She assumes the name "Mitchell" and learns to walk, spit, and scratch like a jock, courtesy of her brother's instruction. Her feminine fingernails bite the dust. Sandy arranges her hair in a goopy pile held together with gel and masking tape. Michelle changes into her uniform before practice—and always wears her helmet.

In the early practices, Michelle finds that last year's kicker "Jocko" Joey isn't happy with the competition, especially once he sees "Mitch" kick so well. He starts to sabotage her efforts by kicking her hand while she holds for him and pointing the laces of the football toward Michelle when she kicks—after he finds out that "Mitch" had never played football before and didn't know that the laces need to face away for the kicker's foot. At the same time, Joey has developed a crush for a "sevie," a (seventh grade girl) he's seen around— school who is none other than Michelle.

The plan begins to fall apart in the second game when a player on the opponent's team returns a kick and gets through Jefferson's defense. Michelle tackles the player to prevent a touchdown. She gets knocked out for a moment and loses her helmet. The discovery of her identity sends everything into a turmoil. The coach is furious—but can't dump her from the team. Michelle unaccountably begins to miss crucial extra points and field goals.

Running through the book are a number of minor plot lines and interesting characters: Miss Ashley Ashleigh, an attractive, assertive home economics teacher; a growing friendship between Matt and Michelle; Joey's heavy-handed crush and jealousy of Matt; the determination of Michelle's mother that she get fair treatment; Sandy's honest reporting, which causes a rift in their friendship; and the meaning of teamwork.

Before the final game, Michelle and Matt discover what Joey has been doing and Michelle's kicking keeps her team close to their archrivals. In the final play of the game, Michelle leads her team to victory with an unexpected play.

Get That Girl Out of the Boys' Locker Room! *(cont.)*

The outline below is a suggested plan for using the various activities and ideas that are presented in this unit. You should adapt these ideas to fit your own classroom situation.

Sample Lesson Plan

Day 1
- Read chapters 1 through 3.
- Conduct SSR (Sustained Silent Reading).
- Discuss Michelle's attitude toward playing on the football team. How does she feel about being compared to a boy by her brother? How do they intend to trick her mother into signing the insurance permission form? What can Michelle do to look and act like a boy?
- Take a Football Survey (Setting the Stage, #3).
- Begin a reading journal (Enjoying the Book, #2).
- Review basic rules of the game (Setting the Stage, #6).
- Write about "Your Favorite Sport" (Setting the Stage, #4).

Day 2
- Read chapters 4 through 6.
- Conduct SSR.
- Discuss Brian's description of how boys act when they are together. Ask students to describe or act out his advice on "being a boy." Discuss Coach Brown's attitude toward Michelle. Discuss the first day of school. Ask students to compare their feelings to Michelle's.
- Continue the reading journal.
- Use pages on Career Choices and Career Goals (Setting the Stage, #7).
- Read The Rules of the Game (Enjoying the Book, #4).
- Learn Football Lingo and Football Terms (Enjoying the Book, #5).

Day 3
- Read chapters 7 through 9.
- Conduct SSR.
- Discuss Joey's attitude toward Mitchell. Did Joey deliberately kick her hand? Should Michelle play with an injury? Discuss Joey's crush on a "sevie." How does Michelle get along with most of the boys on the team? Who does she like best? Why?
- Continue the reading journal.

- Do Where the Action Is (Enjoying the Book, #6).
- Do The Poetry of Football (Extending the Book, #4).

Day 4
- Read chapters 10 through 12.
- Conduct SSR.
- Discuss Michelle's football accident. How do her parents react when they find out the truth? How does Michelle's mother react to Coach Brown's attitude toward girls? Why can't the coach drop her from the team? How is Joey behaving? What is he doing that is peculiar?
- Continue the reading journal.
- Begin football math (Extending the Book, #9).
- Read Girls in the Game and do the comprehension sheet (Extending the Book, #2).
- Introduce writing prompt: Should Girls Play Football? (Extending the Book, #3).

Day 5
- Read chapters 13 through 15.
- Conduct SSR.
- Discuss Michelle's awful game. Does Michelle have a right to be angry at Sandy's critical article? What has Joey been doing to sabotage Michelle's kicks? How does Michelle become a heroine in the concluding chapter? Ask students if they liked the ending.
- Do Elements of a Story (Enjoying the Book, #7).
- Learn more about the author (Extending the Book, #6).
- Read about Becoming an Author (Extending the Book, #7).
- Write poetry (Extending the Book, #5).
- Do Readers' Theater (Extending the Book, #1).
- Write a point of view diary entry (Extending the Book, #11).
- Complete previous writing activities and write a persuasive essay (Extending the Book, #10).
- Do passing and kicking drills (Extending the Book, #12).

Overview of Activities

Setting the Stage

1. Set the mood by asking students to describe the best football game they ever saw or ever played in.

2. Ask each student who plays in any football league or on any school team to make a list of pertinent facts about their team and their league. These facts should include uniforms and sponsors, number of teams, names of the best teams and the best players, specific rules each team must follow, the number of players on each team, who coaches the teams, and playing rules.

3. Conduct a survey of students in your class about the game of football. Use the **Football Survey** form (page 10). Have students complete the table of facts recording the results of the survey. Ask students to create a bar graph to visually express the survey results for favorite sports.

4. Ask students to write one paragraph in response to this prompt: What is your favorite sport? Do you like to play this sport or just watch it? What do you enjoy about this sport? Why does it appeal to you?

5. Before reading the book, ask students to anticipate what the book may be about, judging by the title and the cover.

6. Conduct a general discussion with students about the basic rules of the game of football. Discuss favorite players and teams. Ask students to describe their feelings about the game and the aspects of the game that they like or dislike.

7. Use the **Career Choices** and **Career Goals** work sheets (pages 11 and 12) to encourage students to discern their present interests and to consider careers that may complement those interests. Encourage students to visualize the future by writing their autobiographies after completing the **Career Goal** page.

Enjoying the Book

1. Have students read *Get That Girl Out of the Boys' Locker Room!* over a period of about five days. You may wish to have two half-hour reading periods this week.

2. Ask students to keep a reading journal while they read this book. Each entry should record the number of pages read and list any vocabulary words new to them. Students should record their impressions and reactions to each section. They should respond particularly to some of the opinions expressed by Michelle and indicate whether they agree with her or not.

3. Encourage a discussion of male habits as described by Michelle's brother. Ask students to comment on Brian's advice about walking, spitting, and scratching.

4. Copy and distribute **The Rules of the Game** (pages 13 and 14). Divide the class into two-person teams. Have students in each team alternate in explaining the rules of the game to each other, as if the other student in the pair had no prior knowledge of the game. Students should then switch pairs and repeat the process with the students who listened the first time now doing the explanation. Have students refer to the rules when they are uncertain.

Overview of Activities (cont.)

Enjoying the Book (cont.)

5. Have students do a writing activity by describing a real or imaginary game using the **Football Terms** and **Football Lingo** (pages 46 and 47). Students can also illustrate several figurative expressions from **Football Lingo**. For example: A "hotdog" could be drawn as a football player shaped like a hotdog dressed in uniform and dancing around for the crowd.

6. Review the verbs in **Where the Action Is** (pages 48 and 49) with the students. Instruct students to complete the sentences and do the creative writing activity described. Do **Football's Compound Words** (page 50).

7. Create a chart with the students indicating the elements of a story similar to this outline.

Elements of a Story

Setting of the story
- Where (country/city/rural/school)
- When (time period)

Major characters
- One or two descriptive facts about each one

Lesser characters
- One or two descriptive facts about each one

Plot
- Story line of the book in about 7 to 10 brief sentences

Problem
- What is the basic problem in the book for the main character? Express this problem in one sentence.

Climax
- What one event in the story does everything lead up to and then lead to a resolution?

Ending
- What is the denouement? How does the story end—for the main character, especially?

Feeling
- Is the general tone of the book depressing, uplifting, happy, sad, grim, joyful, funny, light, or serious? Choose the appropriate descriptive words.

Overview of Activities *(cont.)*

Extending the Book

1. Divide the class into teams of four or five students each. Using the **Readers' Theater** (pages 37 through 39), have each team choose a chapter or a scene from *Get That Girl Out of the Boys' Locker Room!* to convert to dramatic format. Then have each drama team present their Readers' Theater to the class.

2. Do the reading comprehension unit entitled: **Girls in the Game** (pages 19 and 20). Encourage students to discuss the reading and the general idea of girls playing football.

3. Ask students to respond to this prompt for a persuasive essay: **Should Girls Play Football?** (page 21). Students should take a position and give arguments and counter-arguments. They can mention examples from youth league and adult leagues as well as from their life experiences or the experiences of others.

4. Do **The Poetry of Football** section (page 40). Assign students a poem to be read in two voices. Allow students several days to practice. Then have each team present their poem to the class.

5. Have students write their own poetry using **Write Your Own Poetry** (pages 41 through 45) to guide students in writing various types of poetry.

6. Use **Focus on an Author** (page 34) to encourage students to read other books by Elaine Moore such as *Who Let Girls in the Boys' Locker Room?*, which has the three girls on the school basketball team.

7. Discuss **Becoming an Author** (page 35) to help students perceive themselves as authors. Help students collect and save a portfolio of their work. Ask them to choose one piece to revise and improve.

8. Have students select another high interest book to read and report (page 36). See the **Bibliography** (page 79) for other choices.

9. Do a unit on football math. Use **Gridiron Computations, Rushing Statistics, Computing Pass Percentages, Comparing Yardage, Calculating Winning Percentages,** and **NFL Salaries** (pages 52 through 57) to reinforce division skills, computing percentages, subtraction, bar graphs, and measurement.

10. Ask students to respond to this prompt for a persuasive essay: Anything you can do, I can do. Should all girls have equal opportunities for jobs and sports as Michelle's mother and Miss Ashleigh clearly believe? Are there any jobs or sports that females would be less able to do? Students should take a strong position and give arguments and counter-arguments.

11. Much of the action in *Get That Girl Out of the Boys' Locker Room!* is told from Michelle's point of view as kicker. Ask students to create a diary of a game—real or imaginary—using point of view. Using **Catch That Game** (page 21), have students write the same entry from the point of view of the quarterback, an opposing defensive player, or even a spectator.

12. Have students read **The Art of Passing** and **Kicking the Ball** (pages 66 and 67). Allow time for students to practice passing and kicking skills in teams of four. Ask students to bring footballs, of any kind, from home or try to borrow several from other teachers.

Football Survey

Directions: Survey all the members of your class using the form below.

What sport do you most like to play?_____

Do you like to play football? _____

Do you like to watch football? _____

What is your favorite NFL team? _____

Who is your favorite NFL player? _____

Have you ever been to an NFL game? _____

Have you ever been to a college football game? _____

Do you play organized football in any league? _____

Would you want to play football when you grow up? _____

Who is the greatest player of all time? _____

Directions: Record the results of your survey on the table below. Then make a bar graph to illustrate the results for the class's favorite sport. Record the sports along the bottom grid. Record the number of students who favor each sport along the side of the grid.

Table of Preferences

Favorite sport

Football_____   Soccer _____

Basketball _____   Other _____

Baseball_____

Like to play football

Yes _____   No _____

Like to watch football

Yes _____   No _____

Favorite NFL team _____

Favorite NFL player _____

Attend NFL games

Yes _____   No _____

Play organized football in any league

Yes _____   No _____

Greatest player of all time _____

Career Choices

Elaine Moore started writing when she was a child. She never gave up her goals.

While sports careers seem attractive and millions of children play football, basketball, baseball, and soccer, only a few hundred actually make it to the NFL or other professional teams. Only a handful of those actually become superstars.

Setting some possible career goals when you are young offers you a greater likelihood of adult success. Use this page to help you discern your personal goals and interests and to help you determine some serious and reasonable career choices.

Personal Interests and Strengths

Do you like to do schoolwork? _____

Why? _____

List three school subjects you like.

_____   _____   _____

List three school subjects you don't like.

_____   _____   _____

List three things you like to read about.

_____   _____   _____

List four interests or hobbies that you do outside of school (stamp collecting, video games, computer use, playing an instrument, reading, writing, etc.).

_____   _____

_____   _____

List four things that you would like to learn how to do (speak a different language, repair cars, play an instrument, play a new sport, take care of animals, etc.).

_____   _____

_____   _____

List three active sports you play alone or on teams.

_____   _____   _____

Do you like to work indoors or out of doors? _____

Do you like to work with your hands? _____

Do you like things to be about the same every day or do you like constant surprises and challenges? Why?

_____

Do you like to work alone or with a group? _____

Who is your hero in life and why? _____

_____

What is your proudest accomplishment? _____

Do you like to draw or paint? _____

What work do you take the greatest pride in doing? _____

Career Goals

List four careers that you think you would like to pursue. Then write two reasons why you think you might like to choose each career. What education would you need for each of these career choices?

Career	Reasons	Education Needed
1.		
2.		
3.		
4.		

Thinking About the Future

When you think about your life as an adult, what images come to mind? In the space below, list or illustrate several personal goals that you may find important (education, house, car, career, etc.).

Your Autobiography

Write your future autobiography from the age you are now until you are thirty years old. Describe your education and training, the early jobs you hope to do on your way to a career, and your life and work as a young adult. Be both realistic about your goals and optimistic that you will achieve them.

The Rules of the Game

Listed here are the rules of the game in simplified format. There are variations in the rules in youth leagues, high school conferences, college football, and the professional leagues.

Object of the Game/Scoring

- The object of the game is to score more points than the other team by moving the ball in the direction of and over the other team's goal line.

- There are four ways to score points—touchdown, extra point, field goal, and safety.

- A touchdown, worth 6 points, is scored by carrying the ball over the other team's goal line or by completing a pass in their end zone.

- After a touchdown is made, one extra point is scored by kicking the ball between the uprights in the other team's end zone. If the ball is carried over the goal line or a pass is completed into the end zone, 2 points are scored. The extra point or conversion is begun from the 2 or 3 yard line, depending on the rules of the league.

- A field goal, worth 3 points, is scored by kicking the ball through the other team's uprights. A field goal is usually attempted if the offensive team is out of downs and fairly close to the defensive end zone.

- A safety, worth 2 points, is scored by tackling a ball carrier in his own end zone.

Playing the Game

- Each team has 11 players on the field.

- After a coin toss to decide which team will receive the ball, one team kicks the ball from a kicking tee to the opposing team.

- The player receiving the ball may carry it until he is tackled, driven out of bounds, or scores by running into the kicking team's end zone.

- A team has 4 plays, called downs, in which to move the ball 10 yards by either carrying the ball or completing passes.

- Each down will start on the line of scrimmage, which is determined by the position of the ball at the end of the last play.

- The team on offense will block for the ball carrier. The team on defense will try to tackle the ball carrier or sack the quarterback before he can throw.

- The end of each play is signaled by the official's whistle.

- If the offensive team moves the ball 10 yards or more, it gets a first down and has four more downs to move the ball another 10 yards.

- A pass that is incomplete or out of bounds does not gain any yardage for the offensive team.

The Rules of the Game *(cont.)*

Playing the Game *(cont.)*

- An offensive team will lose the ball if a player fumbles the ball and it is recovered by the other team.
- An offensive team will lose the ball if it is intercepted by a player on the opposing team.
- If the offensive team fails to gain 10 yards, the offensive team may punt the ball to the other team on the fourth down.
- If the offensive team tries to get the remaining yardage on fourth down and fails, it must turn the ball over to the other team at the position on the field where they are playing. This is a disadvantage to the team that failed to get a first down because it leaves the opposing team closer to the end zone where they are trying to score.
- A ball carrier or receiver who steps out of bounds stops the clock and his forward progress is stopped where he stepped out of bounds.
- A pass does not count as a completed pass if the player catches it having one or both feet out of bounds.

Rule Violations

- A foul is an illegal action on the field. An official usually throws a yellow flag to indicate a foul.
- Fouls include:
    1. holding a player while blocking.
    2. striking an opponent with a fist, foot, forearm, or head.
    3. delay of game by taking too long between plays.
    4. grabbing an opponent's face mask.
    5. defensive interference with a receiver before he catches a pass.
    6. piling on a player after he is down.
    7. roughing the kicker by hitting him after the kick.
    8. too many players on the field.
    9. any unsportsmanlike conduct.

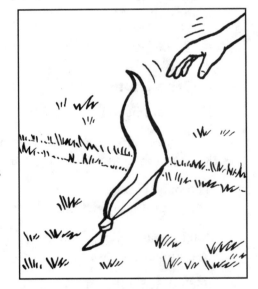

- Fouls result in penalties, which include loss of a down, loss of yardage, or both.

Time and Distance

- The game is divided into four quarters. A quarter may be only 8 minutes for youth leagues. A quarter is 15 minutes in the NFL.
- There is a halftime break of about 15 to 20 minutes.
- Some leagues play an overtime period if the game is tied at the end of four quarters.
- The football field is 100 yards long. The center of the field is the 50 yard line. On each side of the 50 yard line, the numbers decrease and are marked at the 40 yard line, 30 yard line, 20 yard line, 10 yard line, and the goal line.

Formations and Positions

There are many complicated offensive and defensive formations. Formations are the way the 11 players of each team are arranged on the field, waiting for the play to begin. The outline below shows one standard formation. The positions are abbreviated and the full name of each position is listed at the bottom of the page.

- The offense is the team that has possession of the ball and is moving it towards its' goal line.
- The defense is the team that is defending that territory when the other team has possession of the ball.

Offense   **Defense**

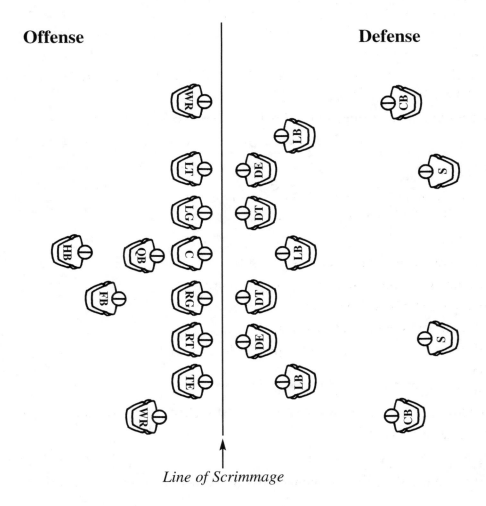

Line of Scrimmage

Player Positions

S–Safety	CB–Cornerback	FB–Fullback
TE–Tight End	DE–Defensive End	LB–Linebacker
LG–Left Guard	DT–Defensive Tackle	LT–Left Tackle
RT–Right Tackle	C–Center	RG–Right Guard
HB–Halfback	QB–Quarterback	WR–Wide Receiver

Formations and Positions *(cont.)*

Other Offensive Formations

T-Formation

(looks like a backwards "T")

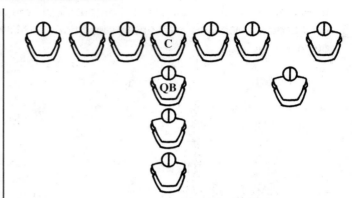

I-Formation

(looks like an "I")

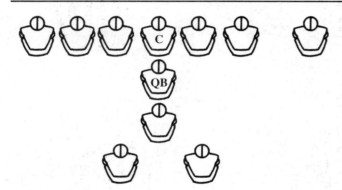

Wishbone Formation

(looks like a "Y" or wishbone)

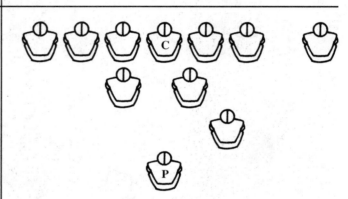

Punt Formation

*(used when the ball will be kicked
to the opposing team)*

Other Defensive Formations

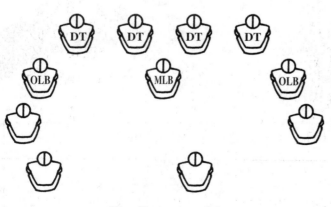

The Four-man Line

(also called the 4-3)

The Three-man Line

(also called the 3-4)

Reading the Signals

Football officials use signs or signals so that players and spectators know when a penalty is being called or a score has been made. Signals are used in all sports to indicate the progress of the game. Here are some of the most important signals used in football.

Directions: Practice these signs with a partner. Have one partner give the sign and the other identify it. Then reverse roles.

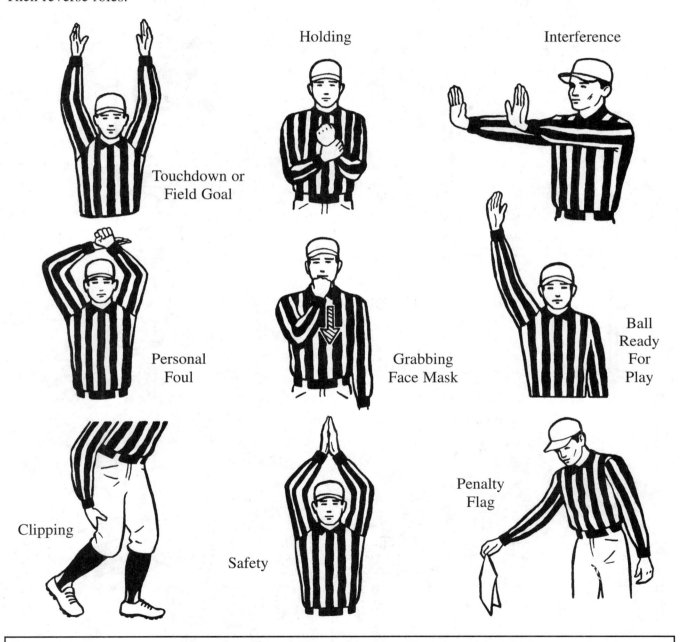

Touchdown or Field Goal

Holding

Interference

Personal Foul

Grabbing Face Mask

Ball Ready For Play

Clipping

Safety

Penalty Flag

Extension

People use all types of signs to communicate. Explore other signs used in other sports; everyday signs or gestures, such as waving to say hello and good-bye; Braille and sign language; and even road signs.

Football Equipment

Football requires a lot of equipment. In addition to a large field, you will also need the following:

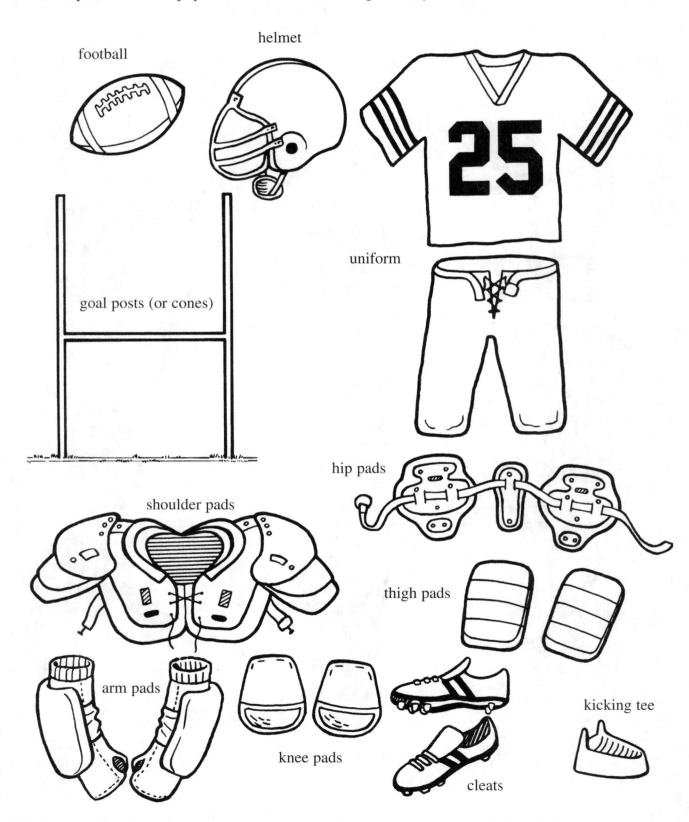

football

helmet

uniform

goal posts (or cones)

hip pads

shoulder pads

thigh pads

arm pads

knee pads

cleats

kicking tee

Girls in the Game

Girls play football, too. In recent years, at least 120 high school girls in the United States played on their schools' male-dominated tackle-football teams. The Women's American Flag Football Federation has member teams all across the United States. Many of these teams play full-contact flag football.

Believe it or not, girls have been playing football in the United States for almost 80 years. In the late 1920s, women's teams were hired by the owners of men's professional teams to play brief games as halftime entertainment during the men's games. Some girls played pickup games with their brothers and friends in local neighborhoods. A women's professional league was started in 1965 but faded within a few years. Another league founded in 1974 dissolved in the early 1980s. There has been a successful American football women's league in Australia since 1987.

The Women's Professional Football League (WPFL) is the latest venture, and it was launched in 1999 with a nationwide barnstorming trip to arouse interest in women's football. The league commenced play in October of 2000 with six teams. Several others are scheduled to be added in the fall of 2002.

The players for women's football are primarily former college athletes who played soccer, rugby, field hockey, basketball, lacrosse, hockey, and other rough-and-tumble contact sports. Some players have also come from fast-pitch softball teams and track and field.

The size of the players varies widely. For example, the New England Storm lists two tailbacks who weigh only 125 pounds. They also have a 250-pound offensive tackle, a player on the defensive line who weighs 290 pounds, and another player on the offensive line who dresses out at 340 pounds. Most of the players weigh in a range from 140 to 190 pounds.

The teams and players on the WPFL hope that their sport will show a dramatic rise in popularity. Teams have appeared on national television shows as well as in pre-Super Bowl festivities. Although their pay is minimal and they travel by inexpensive buses, many fans enjoy the fact that the girls love the game, have time to talk and sign autographs, and especially that they exhibit a full-contact, gritty, action-packed, all-out style of play using NFL rules.

These girls play because they love the game just as much as their fathers, brothers, husbands, and children do. Who knows? In a few years, their games may be as popular as the men's game!

Reading Comprehension Sheet

Directions: Carefully read **Girls in the Game**. Then circle the best answer for each of these questions. Check your work by underlining as many answers in the text as you can find.

1. In what year was the Women's Professional Football League started?
   A. 1965
   B. 1974
   C. 1999
   D. 1980

2. How much do the tailbacks on the New England Storm weigh?
   A. 290 pounds
   B. 125 pounds
   C. 340 pounds
   D. 190 pounds

3. Why were women's teams hired by the owners of men's professional teams in the 1920s?
   A. as replacement players
   B. as coaches
   C. as halftime entertainment
   D. to sell refreshments

4. Women football players are usually recruited from what sports?
   A. contact sports
   B. skiers and skaters
   C. bicyclists
   D. the chess club

5. What football rules are used by teams in the WPFL?
   A. flag football
   B. NFL
   C. touch football
   D. soccer

6. What does the phrase "rough-and-tumble" mean?
   A. not delicate
   B. gentle
   C. neat and tidy
   D. pretty

7. Why do some fans of women's professional football enjoy the game?
   A. the games are on TV
   B. they like to see women's organized teams play
   C. the women play hard
   D. they have better players

8. What does "gritty" mean?
   A. clean and dry
   B. tough and determined
   C. soft and gentle
   D. gray and brown

9. Why did the WPFL arrange a nationwide barnstorming trip?
   A. to see barns
   B. to play against male teams
   C. to catch up with storms
   D. to get publicity

10. According to the story, teams and players in the WPFL have appeared on what types of shows?
    A. The Weather Channel
    B. national television shows
    C. local sport shows
    D. college bowl shows

Should Girls Play Football?

Something to Think About

- In recent years, 120 high school girls in the United States played on their school's tackle-football team, more than 500 played on their high school's baseball team, 120 played ice hockey, and over 200 wrestled in competition with boys.

- In 1971, about a quarter of a million high school girls participated in some athletic program at school. In 1994, more than eight times as many girls participated in a high school sport.

- In the 1996–1997 school year, more than 40% of all high-school athletes were girls.

- About one adult woman out of every three plays a sport.

- About one-third of adult women are interested in the NFL. Almost as many are interested in major league baseball and the NBA.

- The Women's American Flag Football Federation has teams and members who play contact flag football throughout the United States.

Directions

1. Respond to this prompt for a persuasive essay: Should girls play football?

2. The first paragraph should define your position, state your opinions, and give specific reasons and arguments in support of your position. You should use examples from your own life experiences, the experiences of others, and/or games you have played and seen.

3. The second paragraph should deal with counter-arguments to your position. Express what people who disagree with you might say. You should anticipate their opinions, arguments, and examples and respond to these counter-arguments.

4. The concluding paragraph should restate your position and any concluding thoughts.

Catch That Game

We have all seen some sporting event that we played over again in our minds. Sometimes we have changed the game or the score or just one final play. There are even a number of fantasy leagues for sports fans. *Get That Girl Out of the Boys' Locker Room!* and *Catch That Pass!* contain a series of football games seen from the point of view of a player.

Directions: Write your own script of a football game in any situation—school playground, high school, college, or the pros. Place your friends and classmates in the game or use famous players. Include yourself, if you wish. Record the action that occurs, the play of certain individuals, and mention special highlights. Try to make the game interesting, exciting, and action-filled and add a thrilling finish.

Catch That Pass!

by Matt Christopher

Summary

Jim Nardi loves football. He has quick hands, good speed, and the instinct to become an excellent linebacker. He has become skilled at rushing through the offensive line to cover his man and at preventing the quarterback from passing or running the ball. He reacts well in the flux of the game and usually defends against receivers well.

But Jim Nardi has one real fear. He's afraid of being tackled.

He's especially afraid of being tackled at the moment of vulnerability when he leaps up to intercept a pass from the opposition quarterback. He drops these passes. He doesn't hold onto them even when he has them in his hands. He is costing his team, the Vulcans, the chance to win games.

Hook Wheeler, his teammate at left safety, and Dil Gorman, at right safety, are both critical of Jim's play. They let him know that his failure to hold onto intercepted passes has cost the team. They make fun of him in front of the other players on the team. Jim's older brother, Doug, is the Vulcan's coach. He does not directly criticize Jim's play, but he does expect Jim to improve his game.

Jim is very critical of himself. He admits his fear to his little sister, Karen, and to his best friend, Chuckie Gorman. Chuckie was crippled in an automobile accident when he was five and still has to use a wheelchair. Chuckie comes to all of the games to cheer on his friends. He is a very upbeat person who believes that he will someday succeed in walking again. Chuckie loves to race remote-control cars. Dil is his brother, and Jim is his closest friend.

As Jim struggles to overcome his fear, he reaches a point where he considers quitting football, even though he loves the game. The criticism is getting more pronounced and Jim feels that he is letting down the team and his brother, who mentions Jim's dropped interceptions after a loss to the Astrojets.

Three events serve to change his mind. Jim's friend, Bucky, shows Jim a scrapbook with a newspaper clipping of Doug when he was a high school player. The clipping shows that Doug also had to overcome a fear of being tackled and that he succeeded. Jim also burns his arm while putting out a fire in his garage. Although some curtains were burned and he singed his arm, Jim showed quick thinking and good sense in handling the situation. Finally, Jim gets really angry at Hook's insults about his miscues. In the final game against the Saturns, Jim overcomes his fears, makes an interception, and helps the Vulcans achieve second place in their league.

Catch the Pass! *(cont.)*

The outline below is a suggested plan for using the various activities and ideas that are presented in this unit. You should adapt these ideas to fit your own classroom situation.

Sample Lesson Plan

Day 1
- Do Setting the Stage #1–#3.
- Read chapters 1 through 3.
- Conduct SSR (Sustained Silent Reading) (Enjoying the Book, #1).
- Discuss the criticism of Jim's play by Dil and Hook. Does Jim blame himself for the dropped passes? Jim's brother is coaching the team. Would you want to play if your brother or father was the coach? How does Chuckie support Jim? What disability does Chuckie have? Discuss Formations and Positions (Setting the Stage, #4).
- Begin a reading journal (Enjoying the Book, #2).
- Learn football signals (Setting the Stage, #6).
- Talk about football equipment (Setting the Stage, #5).

Day 2
- Read chapters 4 through 6.
- Conduct SSR.
- Discuss Jim's fears and how they affect his play. What is he not afraid of on the field? How does Chuckie help Jim's morale? How does Chuckie show he's a good friend? Does Jim's brother, Doug, know he is afraid?
- Continue the reading journal.
- Start a research report on famous players (Enjoying the Book, #4).
- Read and debate about the Greatest Quarterback and the Greatest Running Back (Enjoying the Book, #5).
- Do Where the Pros Play (Extending the Book, #6).

Day 3
- Read chapters 7 through 9.
- Conduct SSR.
- Discuss how the Vulcans lost the game against the Astrojets. Ask knowledgeable football students to explain the rule against "piling on" a player after a recovered fumble. How does Jim feel when he finds out that his older brother and coach, Doug, had the same fear of being hit when he caught a ball? How does he show quick thinking when a fire starts in his garage?
- Continue the reading journal.
- Start Elements of a Story (Enjoying the Book, #3).
- Do the Knute Rockne comprehension unit (Extending the Book, #1).
- Do What's in a Name? (Extending the Book, #7).
- Research Sports Around the World (Extending the Book, #8).
- Read Football Trivia (Extending the Book, #4).
- Review Exercise and Nutrition (Extending the Book, #11).

Day 4
- Read chapters 10 through 12.
- Conduct SSR.
- Discuss how Jim's burned arm affected his attitude about playing football. Why is he more determined to play and overcome his problems? How did Jim's intercepted pass help Jim prove that he could handle his fear? How does Bucky prove his friendship? Why is Hook always critical of Jim?
- Continue the reading journal.
- Do the College Game (Extending the Book, #5).
- Read and discuss Football Quotes (Extending the Book, #9).
- Encourage students to read other Matt Christopher books (Extending the Book, #2).

Day 5
- Read chapters 13 and 14.
- Conduct SSR.
- Discuss the last two games against the Astrojets and the Saturns. How has Jim matured and become more responsible as a player and a person? How does Jim know that he has overcome his fear? How did Jim's friends, family, and brother help him overcome his fear and become a better player? Who has more courage—Chuckie or Jim?
- Complete Elements of a Story (Enjoying the Book, #3).
- Read Football at School and organize teams (Extending the Book, #14).
- Do Football Chronology (Extending the Book, #10).
- Choose a book to read aloud (Extending the Book, #3).
- Design logos, posters, and uniforms (Extending the Book, #12 and #13).
- Organize Super Bowl Day (Extending the Book, #14).

Overview of Activities

Setting the Stage

1. Before reading the book, ask students to anticipate what the book may be about, judging by the title and the cover.

2. Read the first chapter from *Catch That Pass!* aloud to the class to stimulate interest in the book.

3. Ask students to briefly describe one fear they have had to overcome in life. It may have been the fear of riding a bike, going on a roller coaster, learning a difficult subject, losing a friend or relative, or any similar fear.

4. Ask students familiar with football to diagram on the board some of the formations used in offensive and defensive plays. Use **Formations and Positions** (pages 15 and 16) to help students understand the layout of the game.

5. Go over **Football Equipment** (page 18) to help students become more familiar with the game.

6. Football officials use many signals—so do quarterbacks and defensive players. Using **Reading the Signals** (page 17), have some students model the officials' signs of first down, touchdown, and other plays. Learn about other types of signs and signals used in everyday life.

Enjoying the Book

1. Have students read *Catch That Pass!* during SSR over a period of five days at a rate of about three chapters or 22 pages a day.

2. Expect students to keep a reading journal, as they did with *Get That Girl Out of the Boys' Locker Room!*, while they read this book.

> Each entry should record the following:
> - the number of pages read
> - new vocabulary words
> - impressions and reactions to each chapter section
> - responses to Jim's behaviors and attitudes
> - favorite characters in the book

3. Create a chart with your students indicating the elements of a story similar to the one they did with *Get That Girl Out of the Boys' Locker Room!* Use the outline on page 8.

4. Have students research a famous football player. Use **Research Football Greats** and **Famous Players** (pages 32 and 33) as a guide. Encourage students to become very familiar with the lives of their players. Ask students to give a brief oral report on their players.

5. Complete **The Greatest Quarterback** and **The Greatest Running Back** (pages 29 through 31). Ask students to debate the merits of the players they chose.

Overview of Activities *(cont.)*

Extending the Book

---

1. Have students read **Knute Rockne: The Greatest College Coach** and do the **Reading Comprehension Sheet** (pages 26 and 27). For higher-level comprehension skills, instruct students to underline the part of the reading where each answer is found.

2. Public libraries usually have many copies of the Matt Christopher books. Encourage each student to choose at least one of his books to read in their SSR and homework time. Consider giving a certificate to each child who reads and reports on several of his books. Other Matt Christopher books can be found in the **Bibliography** (page 79).

3. Choose one of the books in **Read!** (page 36) to read aloud to the class. The *Trick* books and *Soup* books make excellent read-alouds, as do most of the books by Matt Christopher and Elaine Moore (page 34).

4. Have students read and comment on **Football Trivia** (page 28). They may have other football anecdotes to relate.

5. Football is a very popular college sport. Use **The United States Map** and **The College Game** (pages 61 and 63) to record the location of each listed college team in the United States.

6. Do the map studies activity and answer the NFL questions in **Where the Pros Play** (pages 60 and 61).

7. Jim Nardi played for the Vulcans, named after the Roman god of fire. Have students do the activities in **What's In A Name?** (page 62)

8. Encourage students to use atlases, encyclopedias, almanacs, the Internet, and other sources to do **Sports Around the World** (page 64). Label the countries and the most popular sport in each country on the **World Map** (page 65).

9. Encourage students to read and discuss **Football Quotes** (page 51) and then do a teaching unit on the proper placement of quotation marks.

10. Review the **Football Chronology** (page 58) with students and then create a corresponding time line with national and international events. Do this on a large chart and help students relate an event to its appropriate time and to a corresponding football event.

11. Review **Exercise** and **Nutrition** (pages 69 and 70). Ask students to maintain an exercise and nutrition log as shown on these pages.

12. Use **Logos and Posters** (page 73) as an art activity. Encourage students to create their own teams. Display the posters on a bulletin board.

13. Ask students to do **Design Your Own Football Uniform** (page 74). They can design a team uniform for any team, professional or made up.

14. Read the pages on **Football at School** (pages 71 and 72).

15. For the culminating activity in this thematic unit, organize a football theme day as described in **Super Bowl** (page 75). Try to get some athletic parents or older students to referee the games. Consider doing a luncheon with parent help based on a football or Super Bowl theme. Be sure to award all participants a **Super Bowl Player Certificate** (page 78) and take plenty of pictures to display on a bulletin board.

Knute Rockne:
The Greatest College Coach

He was born Knute Kenneth Rockne on March 4, 1888, in Norway. His family immigrated to the United States in 1893 and settled in Chicago. Rockne attended Notre Dame University, where he majored in chemistry and graduated in 1914 with the highest honors. It was Rockne's football career, however, which would forever unite his name with Notre Dame's. As a player for Notre Dame, he led his team to an upset victory over Army in 1913. His quick hands caught several passes in this game that brought the forward pass to national attention.

Rockne became the head coach of the Notre Dame football team in 1918. He led his "Fighting Irish" team through 13 seasons during which he amassed 105 victories with only 12 losses and 5 ties. His winning percentage of .881 is the best ever achieved by any coach—college or professional. He won six national championships and coached his team to five undefeated seasons.

"The Rock" helped develop college football into a popular national sport. His innovative approach to the game made it a faster, more action-filled sport and attracted the allegiance of many fans. Rockne was the first college coach to recognize the value of developing intersectional rivalries. He built the first national schedule so that Notre Dame's team was seen in many stadiums throughout the nation.

Rockne's own colorful personality and the style of play he initiated revolutionized the game. Although his players were often smaller than their opponents, they compensated for their lack of size with deceptive moves, finesse plays, and speed. His teams were characterized by exceptional team spirit and gritty determination. They often played bigger and better teams but the cohesiveness of the Notre Dame squad and their fighting spirit made them almost unbeatable.

Rockne coached some of the best and most famous players of the day. George Gipp, Notre Dame's first All-American, was a dazzling player who would run, pass, kick, and lead his team to victory. The "Four Horsemen" were four backfield players who provided the offensive power for Notre Dame between 1922 and 1924. Under their inspired play and Rockne's leadership, Notre Dame won 26 games and lost only two in three years. In their senior year, they went undefeated and beat Stanford for Notre Dame's first national championship.

Rockne was an intensely inspirational leader. Knute's halftime speeches to his team were legendary. The most famous occurred in a game against a powerhouse Army team in 1928. Rockne told his team that George Gipp, while on his deathbed, told him that someday, when Notre Dame is up against long odds, to tell the team to go out and "Win a game for the Gipper." Rockne informed his stunned team "This is the day, and you are the team." A fired-up Notre Dame team went out and beat Army 12–6.

26

Reading Comprehension Sheet

Directions: Read the story about Knute Rockne. After reading each question, circle the letter of the best answer.

1. Which college team did Rockne coach?

   A. Army

   B. Stanford

   C. Chicago

   D. Notre Dame

2. What was Rockne's winning percentage as a college coach?

   A. .881

   B. .891

   C. .262

   D. .818

3. Who were the "Four Horsemen"?

   A. a cowboy team

   B. an Army team

   C. four Notre Dame players

   D. horse riders

4. Why did Knute Rockne tell his players to "Win a game for the Gipper"?

   A. to tell a good story

   B. to catch the four horsemen

   C. to inspire his team

   D. because Gipp was a good player

5. Whom did Notre Dame defeat for their first national championship?

   A. Army

   B. Stanford

   C. Yale

   D. Chicago

6. What country did Rockne's family emigrate from?

   A. Chicago

   B. the United States

   C. Norway

   D. Canada

7. Rockne helped develop intersectional rivalries in football. What does *intersectional* mean?

   A. courageous

   B. between parts of the country

   C. within a state

   D. between two countries

8. What is Notre Dame's nickname?

   A. "the Rock"

   B. "Fighting Irish"

   C. "the Gipper"

   D. "Four Horsemen"

9. How many seasons did Knute Rockne coach at Notre Dame?

   A. 13

   B. 12

   C. 26

   D. 5

10. Rockne's players compensated for their lack of size with deceptive moves, finesse plays, and speed. What does *compensated* mean in this sentence?

    A. built muscles

    B. made up for

    C. paid back a debt

    D. went to another school

Football Trivia

Here are some unusual bits of trivia about the game of football.

- The huddle was invented by deaf students at Gallaudet University in Wahington, D.C., to prevent opposing players from seeing their hand signals.
- In 1905, the game of football had become so dangerous and the players were so poorly protected that at least 19 high school and college football players died from football injuries.
- Usually, between 8 and 12 footballs are used in each NFL game. By comparison Major League Baseball teams use dozens of baseballs in a game.
- The first professional black football player was Charles W. Follis who played for the Shelby team in the Ohio League. One of his teammates was Branch Rickey, who would later bring Jackie Robinson to Major League Baseball.
- Only four NFL Hall of Famers also played major league baseball.
- The 1972 Miami Dolphins had the only perfect, undefeated season in the NFL.
- Numbers were first allowed on the backs of player uniforms in 1915.
- Super Bowl Sunday is the third largest food-eating day for Americans. Thanksgiving and Christmas rank first and second.
- The longest field goal in NFL history was a 63-yard field goal by Tom Dempsey for the New Orleans Saints against the Detroit Lions in 1970. In 1998 Jason Elam of the Denver Broncos equaled the mark against the Jacksonville Jaguars.
- Quarterback Joe Namath of the New York Jets wore pantyhose under his uniform to keep warm on cold game days.
- Supreme Court Justice Byron White was the only member of the court to have played in the NFL.
- President Gerald Ford was offered pro-football contracts to play for the Green Bay Packers and the Chicago Bears. He turned down both offers.
- Footballs are no longer made of pigskin.
- The first legal forward pass was made in a college game in 1906.

Research Trivia

Directions: Use encyclopedias, football books, almanacs, the Internet, and sports magazines to find the answers to the following football questions.

1. What was the "Ice Bowl"? _____
2. What was "The Catch"? _____
3. What was the "Immaculate Reception"?_____
4. When was the first televised football game?_____
5. Who was "Night Train" Lane? _____
6. What was the "Steel Curtain"? _____
7. What is a "redshirted" player?_____
8. Who were the "Four Horsemen" and what were they named after?_____

    _____
9. Who was "The Refrigerator"?_____
10. What is a "Hail Mary" play? _____

28

The Greatest Quarterback

Football fans carry on an endless debate about who was or is the greatest quarterback of all time.

Directions

1. Research the statistics for the three great quarterbacks listed in this section.
2. Read everything else you can find about each quarterback in encyclopedias, magazines, almanacs, other sports books, the Internet, etc.
3. Be prepared to participate in a classroom debate about who was the greatest quarterback. If you wish to choose another quarterback, complete a fact sheet for that player.

Preparing to Debate

- Decide which man you think is the greatest quarterback.
- Make a list of talking points you can use to support your opinion.
- Write one or two paragraphs to summarize your opinions.
- Remember to defend your opinion, listen carefully, speak seriously.

Joe Montana

Football Career

College _____

College statistics _____

Length of time in NFL _____

Teams played for _____

NFL Statistics (Lifetime)

Passes attempted _____

Completed passes _____

Total passing yards _____

Touchdowns _____

Interceptions _____

Average yards per attempted pass _____

NFL quarterback rating points _____

Playoff appearances _____

Super Bowl appearances _____

Career Highlights (great games, special achievements) _____

Influence on the Game (how he changed the game) _____

Personal Characteristics _____

The Greatest Quarterback *(cont.)*

Steve Young

Football Career

College _____

College statistics _____

Length of time in NFL _____

Teams played for _____

NFL Statistics (Lifetime)

Passes attempted _____

Completed passes _____

Total passing yards _____

Touchdowns _____

Interceptions _____

Average yards per attempted pass _____

NFL quarterback rating points _____

Playoff appearances _____

Super Bowl appearances_____

Career Highlights (great games, special achievements)_____

Influence on the Game (how he changed the game) _____

Personal Characteristics _____

Dan Marino

Football Career

College _____

College statistics _____

Length of time in NFL _____

Teams played for _____

NFL Statistics (Lifetime)

Passes attempted _____

Completed passes _____

Total passing yards _____

Touchdowns _____

Interceptions _____

Average yards per attempted pass _____

NFL quarterback rating points _____

Playoff appearances _____

Super Bowl appearances _____

Career Highlights (great games, special achievements)_____

Influence on the Game (how he changed the game) _____

Personal Characteristics _____

The Greatest Running Back

Football enthusiasts also debate the merits of various running backs. Two of the most celebrated are Walter Payton and Emmitt Smith. Use the same process for these players as you did for the quarterbacks. If you choose to do a different running back, make an extra copy for that player.

Walter Payton

Football Career

College _____

College statistics _____

Length of time in NFL _____

Teams played for_____

NFL Statistics (Lifetime)

Rushing attempts _____

Rushing yards _____

Average yards per attempted rush _____

Touchdowns _____

Total yards (including pass receptions) _____

Longest run _____

Playoff appearances _____

Super Bowl appearances_____

Career Highlights (great games, special achievements)_____

Personal Characteristics _____

Emmitt Smith

Football Career

College _____

College statistics _____

Length of time in NFL _____

Teams played for _____

NFL Statistics (Lifetime)

Rushing attempts _____

Rushing yards _____

Average yards per attempted rush _____

Touchdowns _____

Total yards (including pass receptions) _____

Longest run _____

Playoff appearances _____

Super Bowl appearances _____

Career Highlights (great games, special achievements)_____

Personal Characteristics _____

Research Football Greats

Research Guidelines

Directions: Use these guidelines to find important information about your player. Then choose a player from the following page. Use the tips at the bottom of the page to help you write your report.

I. Youth

Birthdate; places lived during youth; family—parents, siblings; home life—(farm/town) (rich/poor) (important events); education—from grade school to high school; activities and hobbies during childhood; childhood heroes

II. Adult Life

Personal Information—marriage/children; college or higher education; adult hobbies and interests

Football Career—years played in college and pro football; positions played; teams played on

Performance—lifetime and best year statistics; special achievements; career highlights; playoff and championship games

Influence on the Game—reputation as a player; what made your player famous?

Greatest Challenge—Did your player have to overcome any obstacles, like injury, illness, learning difficulties, or racism in order to play and succeed at football?

Life After Football—jobs held after playing career in football; coaching career

Personality—Was your player kind, gentle, or tough? Was your player a leader or a follower? How did your player get along with other players, coaches, fans, and officials?

End of Life—date of death (if no longer living); cause of death

III. Personal Evaluation

What do you admire about your player? What was the most interesting thing your player did? What questions would you ask your player?

Research Tips

- *Do the research*—Find out everything you can about your football figure. Discover the important dates, the vital statistics, the personal life, and the struggles of your player.

- *Go to the sources*—Use encyclopedias, almanacs, biographies, the Internet, and other sources of football information to acquire the information you need.

- *Take careful notes*—Use your own words. Write down the basic facts in an orderly way. Look for anecdotes and funny stories about your player. Become familiar with your player's accomplishments.

- *Write your report carefully*—Use your notes to write a detailed account of the life and career of your famous player.

Famous Players

Directions: Select your famous player to research from the list below or choose another player who interests you.

Quarterbacks

Johnny Unitas	great leader; made the Colts the best team of his time
Kurt Warner	an NFL journeyman who won an NFL Championship with the Rams
Roger Staubach	a master of the "two-minute" drill
Joe Namath	"Broadway Joe" pulled off one of the greatest Super Bowl upsets
John Elway	led the Broncos to five Super Bowl appearances
Bart Starr	the Packers' pin-point passer

Running Backs

Jim Brown	tough and dominant; led the NFL in rushing 8 out of 9 years
Gale Sayers	a graceful player with superb balance, instinct, and speed
Barry Sanders	had four straight 1,500-yard seasons and 10 straight 1,000-yard seasons
Eric Dickerson	holds record for most yards rushing in a season (2,130)
Marshall Faulk	currently considered the best running back in the NFL; great pass catcher
Franco Harris	"Mr. Consistency" for the Steelers

Receivers

Jerry Rice	simply the greatest receiver ever; holds most single-season and career receiving records
Raymond Barry	ran his patterns perfectly; was Unitas' favorite receiver
Lynn Swann	graceful and acrobatic; star of Super Bowl X
Cris Carter	made the "big catches" when it counted; known for his catches along the sidelines and in the back of the end zone
Don Hutson	helped make the forward pass an NFL weapon

Defensive Players

David Jones	this "Deacon" invented the sack
Reggie White	all-time leader in sacks
Joe Greene	anchored Pittsburgh Steelers' "Steel Curtain"
Merlin Olsen	went to the Pro Bowl 14 out of 15 years
Dick Butkus	fierce, imposing middle linebacker
Ronnie Lott	great cornerback and safety, known for his vicious tackling

Coaches

Tom Landry	head coach for the Cowboy for 29 years
Don Shula	the winningest coach in NFL history
Vince Lombardi	his name became synonymous with total effort
Bear Bryant	led Alabama's Crimson Tide for decades
Pop Warner	one of the founder of the game

Focus on an Author: Elaine Moore

You can always tell when Elaine Moore is writing and doesn't want to be disturbed. She'll be wearing her purple writer's hat. She started the habit to warn her family that she was working and didn't want to be distracted by her teenage daughters. It has become Elaine's trademark that she wears when speaking at workshops, conventions, and more than 500 schools.

Elaine Moore started developing her writing skills at a very early age using crayons. Then she graduated to pencils. She got a major boost when she had to babysit her little sister. Elaine discovered that she could keep her rather willful sister under control by writing stories with cliff-hanging chapter endings that Elaine would only read to her sister on Friday nights—if she had been good for Elaine all week. Elaine got her sister to do her own chores and Elaine's as well and learned the marvelous power of a well-told story.

Elaine Moore's books often deal with her own experiences. *Grandma's House* highlights the special love Elaine felt for her maternal grandmother. The main character, Kim, loves summer best because she gets to spend time with her grandmother each summer. In *Grandma's Promise*, *Grandma's Garden*, and *Grandma's Smile*, she explores the other three seasons with her grandmother. *Deep River* is the story of Jesse's first fly-fishing trip with her grandfather.

Mixed-Up Sam features a purring dog, a barking cat, and a family with an upside-down way of life. *I'd Rather Be Eaten by Sharks* is a clever story of a child who has to write and deliver an oral report in class. The reader also learns some public speaking tips.

Elaine Moore often conducts workshops in schools where she collaborates with students in writing stories and takes them through the difficult process of revision. She collaborated with some of her students in writing *The Substitute Teacher from Mars*, a story about a group of students trying to get into the *Guinness Book of Records* for having the most substitute teachers in one year. The principal brings in the substitute teacher from Mars to restore order.

Who Let Girls in the Boys' Locker Room! describes how Michelle, Skye, and Keisha join the boys' basketball team. Laced with a good deal of humor and a serious story of basketball competition, the books deals with the meaning of teamwork and the value of friendship. The sequel to this book is *Get That Girl Out of the Boys' Locker Room!*.

Elaine Moore continues to write and to encourage young people to become writers. You can learn more about this author by visiting her web site at *http://www.elainemoore.com*.

Becoming an Author

Keep a Journal

Many authors keep journals for recording their daily experiences. This journal may be in a diary format or just a spiral binder. Some authors simply tell what happened to them that day or note important things they don't want to forget. Other authors jot down ideas or themes that come to mind. Some writers record descriptions of people, places, or landscapes that appeal to them and which they may sometime use. Those with an interest in nature may keep verbal and artistic sketches of plants, animals, or other natural objects.

Keep Your Work

Keep all of your writing for each year in a separate folder. Include everything you wrote that has a creative element to it. Include all of your essays, stories, and compositions. Use paper fasteners and a sturdy cover to secure your work. Compare what you've written this year with folders of your earlier school years. Can you see how your work has matured?

Revise

Elaine Moore spends a great deal of time and effort revising her manuscripts. She tightens the language, plays with the dialogue to make it more realistic, searches for exact words to express her meaning, and tries to make the story flow for the reader. All good writers do the hard work of revision. Choose a story you have written and then revise it keeping the following in mind:

1. Look for simple, weak verbs such as "is, had, said, ran, did, and wanted" and replace them with stronger verbs such as "rushed, fled, sweated, pleaded, and stammered."

2. Begin your story with a good lead—one that grabs your readers' attention and holds it.

3. Add details, which you may have ignored in your first draft.

4. Make the story flow smoothly from paragraph to paragraph. Be sure each paragraph sticks to one topic. Make sentence and paragraph transitions clear.

5. Check for periods, capitals, commas, and other important symbols. Make sure paragraphs are indented and margins are neat.

6. Do a final copy that is legible, and interesting to the reader.

Write . . . Write . . . Write . . .

Good authors write—all of the time. Develop your own style of writing and your own interests by writing about things other than class assignments.

- **Write What You Know**

  If you know football, basketball, or baseball, write a sports article reviewing a recent game that you watched. If you go fishing or roller blading, write about these subjects. Other topics might include cooking, television stars, popular musicians, fixing a bicycle, or a beloved pet.

- **Old Stories . . . with a New Twist**

  Consider rewriting a famous story using the characters from the original story but changing the story entirely or by inserting an ending which you prefer. You might choose to rewrite a chapter of *Get That Girl Out of the Boys' Locker Room!* by adding a different ending.

Read!

Good writers read—all of the time. One of the best ways to improve your writing is to read books and series by good authors.

The series of books highlighted on this page are well written and they are highly appealing to most children. The books mentioned here and other books in the series are listed in the **Bibliography** (page 79).

Soup

The best football player in the *Soup* books is Janice Riker. She is also the toughest kid in the neighborhood. "Soup" is the nickname for the title character in the series. Not only does Soup manage to get into tons of difficult scrapes but she always manages to get his best friend, Rob, involved, too. The author is Robert Newton Peck (Rob in the stories) and they are clearly based on experiences from his childhood. *Soup for President* details a class election with an unexpected ending. *Soup's Drum* is based on a town band with more instruments than talent. *Soup & Me* is a series of vignettes including a runaway pumpkin at a Halloween party.

The Great Brain

The Great Brain in this series of books by John D. Fitzgerald is the author's younger brother, Tom. The setting is the late 1890s in Utah, a time and an area which is just beginning to emerge from frontier conditions. *The Great Brain* commences with the construction of an indoor toilet in the family home. This is the first of its kind in the area, and Tom decides to charge the neighborhood kids admission to see it—until his mother interferes. In *The Great Brain at the Academy*, Tom tries to convince his high school principal to allow the newly invented game of basketball to be played. He also manages to acquire a large number of demerits, to run an illegal candy store, and to get the better of a school bully.

The Hockey Trick

A chemistry set is at the center of the *Trick* books by Scott Corbett. No matter what Kirby and Fenton try to do, something seems to go awry. In *The Hockey Trick*, a potion makes the puck swerve from one stick to another—but their team still doesn't win. In *The Home Run Trick*, they can't even lose a game that they don't want to win. In *The Hairy Horror Trick*, the boys acquire a beard and a mustache and can't get rid of them. *The Turnabout Trick* features a cat that barks and a dog that acts very feline.

The Matt Christopher Books

The sports fiction of Matt Christopher includes a number of football books with a lot of action and a problem to be solved. *Football Fugitive* describes one boy's desire to have his father get involved in his games. *Football Nightmare* details one player's failure to catch a game-winning pass and how he overcomes his failure. *Tough to Tackle*, *Long Arm Quarterback*, and *The Team That Couldn't Lose* are among the football titles written by this sports writer. Matt Christopher has also written many books with baseball and basketball themes. His subjects even include soccer, hockey, and skateboarding.

Readers' Theater

Readers' Theater is drama without costumes, props, stage, or memorization. It is done in the classroom by groups of students who become the cast of the dramatic reading.

Staging

Your classroom is the stage. Place four or five stools in a semicircle at the front of your class or in a separate staging area. If you have no stools, have students sit on the tops of desks, facing the audience. Students may use simple costumes like hats, coats, or football uniform tops but generally no costume is expected or used in this type of dramatization.

If you have plain robes or simple coats of the same color or style so that everyone looks about the same, this can have a nice effect. Students dressed in the same school uniform, team uniform, or colors create an atmosphere of seriousness. Props are not needed, but they may be used for additional details.

Scripting

Readers' Theater can be done using a standard play format. It is also easy to convert well-written dialogue from children's literature into a dramatic format.

Keep the number of actors to four or five at the most. The most important reader with the largest amount of text is the narrator. You can easily have the narrator role divided between two actors, if the text is long.

If you pick a children's book, such as *Catch That Pass!* or *Get That Girl Out of the Boys' Locker Room!*, find a selection with a good deal of exciting or interesting dialogue.

- Assign the narrator to the sections without quotes.
- Assign separate actors to each role in the dialogue, such as Jim, Doug, Hook, Chuckie, Michelle, Brian, or Skye. If there are too many roles, have one actor do two parts. (Make sure these two parts don't have to talk to each other.)
- Drop the inter-dialogue remarks such as "he said," "answered Jim," or "grumbled Hook."
- Copy the text so that each child has a clearly marked, usable script.
- Place scripts in folders that are uniform in color and size.
- Allow children to practice several times over several days before presenting in front of the class.

Performing

Students should enter quietly and seriously into a dimly lit room, with the scripts held in the same position. Actors should sit silently and unmoving on the stools or desks and wait with head lowered or alternatively focusing on a point above the audience such as a clock. The narrator should start reading and the actors will then focus on their scripts. The actors should focus on whoever is reading, except when they are performing.

Extensions

Encourage students to add movement and memorization to performances after they have had several experiences in Readers' Theater. They can introduce mime to the performance and add props or costumes, as the circumstances allow. Some students may begin to add accents as they become more familiar with the drama.

Readers' Theater *(cont.)*

Readers' Theater Activities

1. Convert one of these sections from *Get That Girl Out of the Boys' Locker Room!* to a script for Readers' Theater.
2. Practice reading the scripts with the group for several days.
3. Present the Readers' Theater to your class audience.
4. Choose other sections throughout the book with three to six speakers.

Selections from *Get That Girl Out of the Boys' Locker Room!*

From the middle of page 11 to the middle of page 17

Dialogue and gestures as Michelle gets invited to join the football team

- Use six actors: Narrator, Michelle, Sandy/Skye, Brian, Derek/Lamar, Rani, and Matt.
- Write a brief narrator's introduction for page 11.

Pages 20 through 22

Phone conversation between Michelle and Matt

- Use three actors: Narrator, Matt, and Michelle.
- Write a brief narrator's introduction for page 20.

Pages 27 through 33

Planning meeting to get Michelle on the team

- Use seven actors: Narrator, Michelle, Sandy, Skye, Brian/Derek, Rani/Lamar, and Matt.
- Write a brief narrator's introduction for page 27.

Pages 39 through 41

Learning to act like a boy

- Use three actors: Narrator, Brian, and Michelle.
- Write a brief narrator's introduction for page 39.

From the bottom of page 42 to the middle of page 45

Fixing Michelle's hair

- Use three actors: Narrator, Sandy, and Michelle.
- Write a brief narrator's introduction for page 41.

Pages 47 through 53 (chapter 5)

First practice

- Use five actors: Narrator, Sandy, Matt, Coach Brown, and Michelle.
- Write a brief narrator's introduction for page 47. Condense the story a little.

From the bottom of page 67 through page 72

Practice with Joey

- Use three actors: Narrator, Joey, Coach Brown, and Michelle.
- Write a brief narrator's introduction for page 67 and description of the kicking on the following pages.

38

Readers' Theater *(cont.)*

Converting Stories to Drama

You can write and perform your own Readers' Theater scripts using the following suggestions:

- Watch two good intramural football teams play against each other for a few minutes at school during recess or P.E. or watch a junior high or high school game between two schools. You could also watch part of a televised college or NFL game.

- Take notes of the action that occurs. Be sure to describe the players and the positions they play. Use all of the football language that you can to describe the action on the field. Describe the way the quarterback and his fellow players work together and if they seem to have practiced and played a good deal together. If the real game is not exciting enough, create an imaginary game with real or imaginary players. Be sure to fill the story with plenty of action and to make the game tight and exciting. Use **Football Terms** (page 46) and **Football Lingo** (page 47) to help you.

- Convert this creative writing activity to a script with two announcers. You may adopt the names of real announcers or make up your own names, teams, television or radio station, players, and football stadiums. Feel free to add commercials and interviews with players and fans.

- You will need two main readers for the announcers and one or two other readers for the fans, players, commercials, and other commentary. You might want to add props, such as fake microphones, or add sounds to heighten the realism of the game.

Converting Other Books

Choose a chapter, with several characters and a lot of dialogue, from one of your favorite books. Use a narrator for the basic introduction and text and different readers to do the dialogue. Remember to drop the "he said's" and other unimportant words. The following books work well for this project:

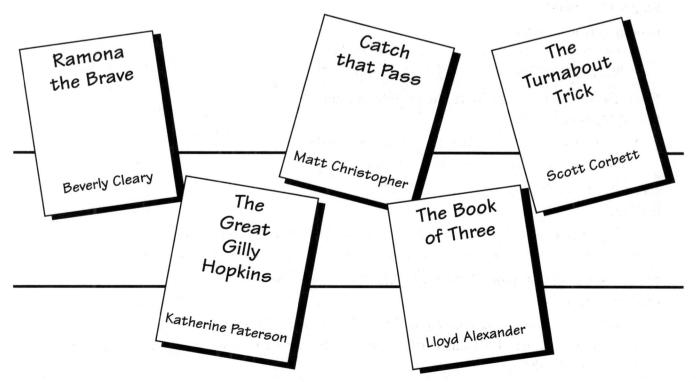

Ramona the Brave — Beverly Cleary

Catch that Pass — Matt Christopher

The Turnabout Trick — Scott Corbett

The Great Gilly Hopkins — Katherine Paterson

The Book of Three — Lloyd Alexander

The Poetry of Football

Read the football poem entitled "Ties," by Dabney Stuart, to the class. It is included in a collection of sports poems entitled *Opening Days*. Then read "In The Beginning Was The" by Lillian Morrison from a collection entitled *Celebrate America in Poetry and Art*. Ask your students to compare the two poems and give their impressions.

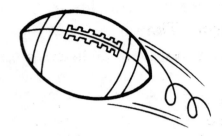

Poetry in Two Voices

An effective way to make poetry dynamic is to encourage two children to recite the poem together. They may recite alternate verses for part of the poem and recite some sections together as a choral reading.

This technique can be used with any of the sports poems from *Opening Days* or the poems from *Celebrate America* as well as other children's poems you know. You might want to use the color poems from *Hailstones and Halibut Bones*. The *Oxford Illustrated Book of American Children's Poems* has a number of excellent pieces by poets such as Sarah J. Hale, Emily Dickinson, Vachel Lindsay, Eve Merriam, and Shel Silverstein.

Other effective poems include "O Captain! my Captain!," "Barbara Fritchie," "The Highwayman," "Eldorado," and "The Walrus and the Carpenter." For poems which are already written to be read in two voices, try Paul Fleishman's Newbery Award winning *Joyful Noise*, a collection of poems about insects.

Poetry in Two Voices

Directions

1. Choose a partner.

2. Choose a poem from the collection your teacher has provided. Pick a poem that appeals to you because of the rhythm or subject matter.

3. Divide up the poem into parts so that you and your partner can recite the poem back and forth. Practice reciting together so that you have the same speed, volume, and pace.

4. Recite the poem for the class.

Student Partners: _____

Poem Chosen: _____

We will practice and recite our poem on _____

                                                          (date)

Signatures: _____

Write Your Own Poetry

Rhyme Time

Directions: Complete these lists of rhyming words.

game	blows	old	corn
lame	nose	cold	born
blame	toes	fold	worn
_____	_____	_____	_____
_____	_____	_____	_____

scored	shot	skate	flat
soared	plot	wait	slat
sword	slot	great	mat
_____	_____	_____	_____
_____	_____	_____	_____

smash	play	run	blues
trash	fray	fun	bruise
flash	clay	sun	clues
_____	_____	_____	_____
_____	_____	_____	_____

wood	style	right	tried
could	trial	bright	glide
would	file	quite	slide
_____	_____	_____	_____
_____	_____	_____	_____

ball	thrill	hope	stare
stall	still	rope	dare
crawl	skill	soap	wear
_____	_____	_____	_____
_____	_____	_____	_____

seek	numb	pack	jump
reek	thumb	stack	bump
weak	some	back	stump
_____	_____	_____	_____
_____	_____	_____	_____

Write Your Own Poetry *(cont.)*

Rhyme Time *(cont.)*

Directions: Use the list of words you completed on page 41 to make rhyming poems similar to the ones illustrated here. Try doing some that have 8 or 12 lines.

- ***All end words rhyme***

  Who's holding the ball?

  He doesn't look very tall.

  I don't care if I'm small.

  Even the big ones fall.

  _____

  _____

  _____

  _____

- ***Alternating rhyme***

  I've got the deep, dark blues.

  Football is my favorite game.

  Upon my toe I got a bruise.

  That made my foot go lame.

  Next time I'll wear my shoes.

  I've only got myself to blame.

  _____

  _____

  _____

  _____

  _____

  _____

Directions: Finish the following poems. Then use another sheet of paper to write more poems of your own.

I just love to roller skate.

I don't care if I'm too late

_____

_____

My best friend does jumping jacks

While I try to miss all the cracks.

Blowing bubbles and skipping rope

She skips on down the cement slope.

_____

_____

_____

_____

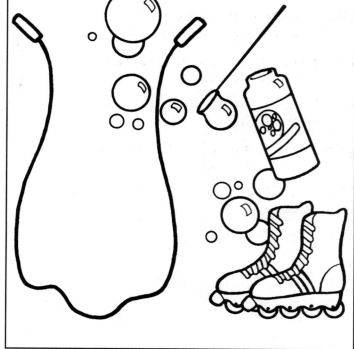

Write Your Own Poetry *(cont.)*

Pigskin Poetry

These poems are similar to cinquains and diamante. They follow a specific pattern and are arranged in a football-like shape.

Directions: Study the examples below. Then write your own pigskin poetry on a sheet of paper. Consider using football or another favorite sport as the subject of one of the poems.

Example

Pattern One

Line 1—one word (*noun, title of the poem*)

Line 2—two words (*adjectives, description*)

Line 3—three words (*expressing feeling*)

Line 4—two words (*verbs ending in -ing*)

Line 5—summation (*noun*)

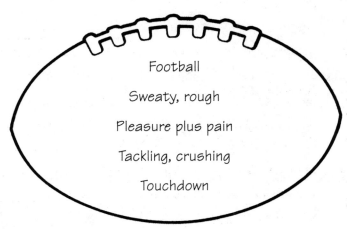

Football

Sweaty, rough

Pleasure plus pain

Tackling, crushing

Touchdown

Example

Pattern Two

Line 1—one word (*noun, title and subject of the poem*)

Line 2—two words (*adjectives, description*)

Line 3—three words (*verbs ending in either -ing or -ed but not both*)

Line 4—four words (*expressing feeling, can be a sentence*)

Line 5—three words (*adverbs, describing the verbs*)

Line 6—two words (*adjective/noun phrase related to subject*)

Line 7—one word (*adjective or interjection, summation*)

Pass

High, deep

Spiraling, soaring, spinning

Please catch the ball!

Wobbly, tipsily, rapidly

Incredible catch

Wow!

Write Your Own Poetry *(cont.)*

I like . . .

The formula for this type of poetry is to add a descriptive word to each line, making the final line the summation. These poems can help develop descriptive vocabulary and rhyme.

Example

I like football.

I like tough football.

I like tough, grinding football.

I like tough, grinding football in the rain.

I like tough, grinding football in the muddy rain.

I like tough, grinding football in the muddy, mucky rain.

I like tough, grinding football in the muddy, mucky, driving rain.

Directions: Write two "I like . . ." poems about football, another sport, or any topic you like.

I like _____.

I like _____ _____.

I like _____ _____ _____.

I like _____ _____ _____ _____.

I like _____ _____ _____ _____ _____.

I like _____ _____ _____ _____ _____ _____.

I like _____ _____ _____ _____ _____ _____ _____.

I like _____.

I like _____ _____.

I like _____ _____ _____.

I like _____ _____ _____ _____.

I like _____ _____ _____ _____ _____.

I like _____ _____ _____ _____ _____ _____.

I like _____ _____ _____ _____ _____ _____ _____.

Write Your Own Poetry *(cont.)*

I wish . . .

The formula for this type of poetry is to write a wish on the first line. The rest of the poem is based on this wish. This type of poem has a very flexible format.

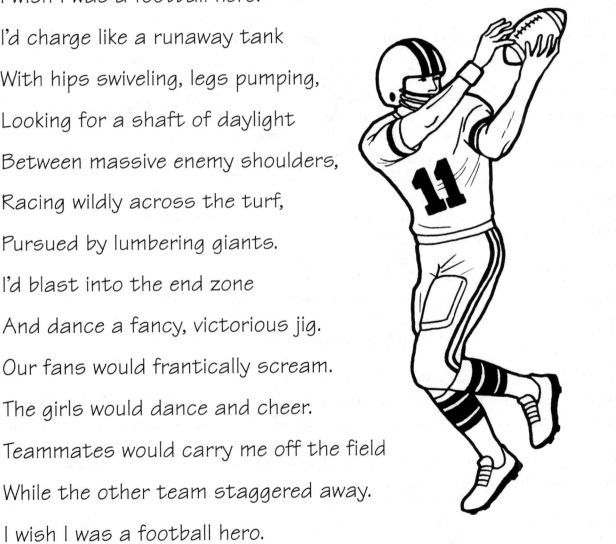

I wish I was a football hero.

I'd charge like a runaway tank

With hips swiveling, legs pumping,

Looking for a shaft of daylight

Between massive enemy shoulders,

Racing wildly across the turf,

Pursued by lumbering giants.

I'd blast into the end zone

And dance a fancy, victorious jig.

Our fans would frantically scream.

The girls would dance and cheer.

Teammates would carry me off the field

While the other team staggered away.

I wish I was a football hero.

Directions: Create your own "I wish . . . poems." Use a football or sports topic or choose something else you especially like.

Football Terms

Directions: On another sheet of paper, use the following terms to describe the action in a play-by-play account of one quarter of a football game. Try to use 15 terms.

audible   a different play called out in code at the line of scrimmage by the quarterback

block   an offensive player makes contact with a defensive player to keep him away from the quarterback or ball carrier

center   the player in the middle of the offensive line who snaps the ball to the quarterback

defensive linemen   the defensive players on the line of scrimmage who rush the quarterback to sack him or to stop the progress of a ball carrier

down   a play run by the offensive team from the line of scrimmage; a team must move the ball 10 yards within four downs or surrender it to the other team

extra point   also called a conversion, a point made after a touchdown by kicking the ball between the goal posts above the bar; two extra points can be made by running or passing the ball into the end zone

fair catch   a signal made by the receiver of a punted ball that he intends to catch the ball; he cannot run with the ball or be hit by the opposing team

field goal   a three-point play made by kicking the ball between the goal posts above the crossbar

formation   the arrangement of the 11 players at the beginning of a play

forward pass   a ball thrown forward from behind the line of scrimmage to another player

foul   breaking the rules, signified by an official throwing a yellow flag during a play

fullback   an offensive player who often blocks for the quarterback or halfback but can also run with the ball or catch a pass

fumble   when a player drops a football he had possession of

halfback   sometimes called a tailback or a running back, an offensive player who lines up behind the quarterback and runs with the ball, receives passes, or blocks for a teammate

hand off   to hand the ball to another player

huddle   a group of players receiving instructions for the next play

incomplete pass   a forward pass not caught by an offensive player or intercepted by a defensive player

kickoff   the start of the game where one team kicks the ball to the other team

line of scrimmage   the imaginary line that separates the offensive team from the defensive team; the ball is put in play from this line

offside   an infraction where a player crosses the line of scrimmage before the ball is snapped to the quarterback

penalty   a loss of downs or yards assessed for breaking a rule

quarterback   the offensive team leader who calls the plays

receiver   a player who catches a pass

tackle   to bring down a player who is holding the ball

touchdown   six points scored by carrying the ball into or catching the ball within the opponent's end zone

Football Lingo

Directions: Read the following figurative expressions and their meanings. Then use some of them in your poetry writing or choose some of them to illustrate (cartoons are effective) on another sheet of paper. For example, for a coffin corner, you could draw a few coffins in the corner of a football field.

birdcage	the facemask with extra horizontal and vertical bars
blind side	to hit a player from the direction opposite from which he is looking
blitz	a full speed defensive charge to hit the quarterback
bootleg	a fake hand off to a runner going one way while the quarterback runs or passes to the other side
clip	to illegally hit a player's leg from behind
coffin corner	one of the corners of the field where the punter tries to kick the ball to prevent an effective run-back
cut	to make a quick move to avoid a pursuing player
gridiron	the football field
Hail Mary	a long, desperation throw by a losing team's quarterback to try to score a touchdown
hitch and go	a move by a receiver who fakes a catch and runs farther down field
hotdog	a showboat player who shows off for the camera
mousetrap	allowing a defensive player through the line so he can be blocked by another player
nose guard	the center defensive player lining up opposite the offensive center
pigskin	another name for a football
piling on	jumping onto a player after he's been tackled
pocket	the area where the quarterback throws from while he is protected by blockers
red dogging	a blitz (several defensive players rush the quarterback at once)
sack	to knock down the quarterback before he can get rid of the ball
safety valve	a short pass from the quarterback when he can't find another receiver
scramble	when a quarterback runs to get away from tacklers
snap	handing the ball from the center to the quarterback
spearing	hitting another player with the head
straight arm	also called a stiff arm; to jab a stiff arm at an opposing player to avoid being tackled
suicide squad	kick off coverage units that go full out on certain plays and suffer a high injury rate

Where the Action Is

Verbs describe the action in a sentence. Football announcers use many exciting and descriptive verbs to paint word pictures of the action on the field.

- The *present form* (present tense) is used to describe action now. **Example:** *I **punt** the ball.*
- The *past form* (past tense) is used to describe action that happened already. **Example:** *I **punted** the ball.*
- The *continuing form* (present participle) is used to describe action which is still occurring. **Example:** *I am **punting** the ball.*

Directions: Complete the chart with the missing letters and words. Look for the patterns. Use a dictionary to check your answers.

Present	Past	Continuing
punt	punted	punting
block	blocked	blocking
intercept	intercept _____	intercept _____
sack	sack _____	sacking
encroach	encroached	encroaching
pass	passed	pass _____
rush	_____	_____
ricochet	ricocheted	ricocheting
kick	_____	_____
squirt	_____	_____
smash	_____	_____
blitz	blitz _____	blitz _____
crush	_____	_____
launch	_____	_____
unload	_____	_____
smash	_____	_____

For verbs ending in *e*, drop the *-e* and add *-ed* to the past form and *-ing* to the continuing form.

fake	faked	faking
spike	spike _____	spik _____
scramble	scrambled	scrambling
tackle	tackl _____	tackl _____
fumble	_____	_____
huddle	_____	_____
explode	_____	_____

For verbs ending in a vowel and consonant, double the final consonant before adding *-ed* or *-ing*.

clip	clipped	clipping
ram	rammed	ramming
slam	slam _____	slam _____

Some verbs are formed irregularly.

catch	caught	catching
drive	drove	driv _____
sweep	swept	sweep _____

Where the Action Is *(cont.)*

Directions: Complete each sentence using one of the verbs listed on page 48. Use the clues in the sentence to find the verb with the most appropriate meaning for the sentence. Use a dictionary, if needed.

1. Jerry Rice _____ the ball into the ground after he made a touchdown.

2. Tom Dempsey _____ the ball through the uprights for a 63-yard field goal.

3. Cris Carter was _____ for the ball carrier to help him score.

4. Steve Young was _____ the ball to his wide receiver.

5. The linebacker hit the quarterback and _____ him for a 10-yard loss.

6. The defensive lineman _____ an offensive blocker when he hit him from behind and below the knees.

7. All of the linebackers and defensive backs are _____ the quarterback to make him get rid of the ball.

8. The quarterback _____ a pass in one direction and ran the other way.

9. The defensive player is _____ the halfback and trying to bring him to the ground.

10. A defensive player is over the line of scrimmage and touching an offensive player before the snap and is _____ on the offensive team.

Extension

Create two football teams with several players. They can be real players, classmates, or famous people. Use the verb list to describe how each player moves and acts during one down. Describe what he does from the huddle to the end of the play. Organize your writing by listing the team, player name, position, and action for each player. Write one or two sentences for each player.

Football's Compound Words

Spelled Apart

blind side	goal line	first down
chain crew	line of scrimmage	option play
coffin corner	first and ten	pump fake
check off	game ball	piling on
face mask	hang time	play action
coin toss	field goal	punt return
delay of game	hand off	tight end
draw play	onside kick	suicide squad
extra point	hitch and go	wide receiver
end zone	forward pass	

Spelled Together

bootleg	touchdown	kickoff
birdcage	football	runback
buttonhook	hotdog	touchback
clothesline	gridiron	tailback
crackback	mousetrap	uprights
backfield	linebacker	cornerback
fullback	offside	kneepads
quarterback	pigskin	crossbar
halfback	overtime	goalpost
lineman	playbook	sidelines

Hyphenated

place-kick	post-season	T-formation
goal-line stand	pre-season	I-formation

Directions: Use the compound words from these lists to complete the sentences below. They can also be used for other writing activities.

1. Another word for football is _____ .

2. The _____ starts a football game.

3. The offense took too long to put the ball in play and was penalized for _____ .

4. The _____ caught a long pass and ran for a touchdown.

5. The field goal kicker drove the ball directly through the _____ above the _____ .

6. The halfback took a _____ from the quarterback.

7. The special teams units are sometimes called the _____ because they have a higher rate of injuries.

8. The fullback ran 10 yards for a _____ on the 17-yard line.

9. The _____ decides which team gets to receive the ball first in a game.

10. If one player hits a ball carrier after the whistle blows, he will be penalized for _____ .

50

Football Quotes

More than a century of football has left fans with many great lines about the game and its players. Here are a few interesting quotes.

"If a man watches three football games in a row, he should be declared legally dead."—**Erma Bombeck**

"Football features two of the worst aspects of American life: violence and committee meetings."—**George Will**

"We didn't lose the game; we just ran out of time."—**Vince Lombardi,** *legendary Packers coach*

"Football is blocking and tackling. Everything else is mythology."
—**Vince Lombardi**

"Only three things can happen when you put a ball up in the air—and two of them are bad."—**Duffy Daugherty,** *college coach*

"A tie is like kissing your sister."—**Bear Bryant**, *famed Alabama coach*

"A winner never whines."—**Paul Brown**, *NFL coach and owner*

"One man practicing sportsmanship is far better than a hundred teaching it."
—**Knute Rockne**, *legendary Notre Dame coach*

Working with Quotations

- Quotations are used to identify the exact spoken words of a speaker.

- Quotation marks are placed before the first spoken word and after the last spoken word.

- Quotation marks are not used around the words which identify who said it or how it was said.

   "In football, the object is to march into enemy territory and cross his goal. In baseball the object is to go home," said George Carlin, mockingly.

- Broken quotes have quotations around the spoken words separated by who said it.

   "Football is to baseball as blackjack is to bridge," said Vin Scully. "One is the quick jolt; the other the deliberate, slow-paced game of skill."

Directions: Go to any event—a football game or even a movie. Ask spectators for their comments on the game or reactions to the movie. Record their exact words using quotation marks. Tell who said each comment and how it was said.

Gridiron Computations

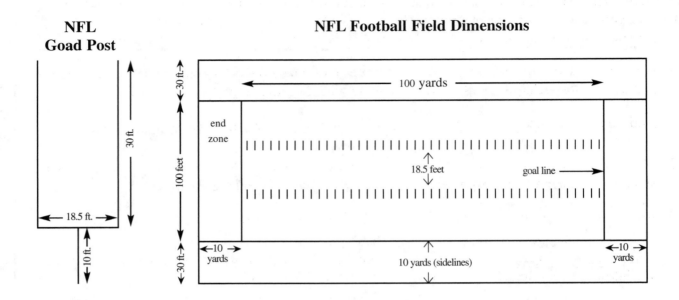

NFL Goad Post

NFL Football Field Dimensions

Directions: Use the information on this page and the formulas to solve these word problems.

Formulas: area of a rectangle = *length* x *width*

perimeter of a rectangle = (*length* + *width*) x 2

1 yard = 3 feet

1. What is the length of the football field in feet? _____

2. What is the length of the football field in feet, including both end zones? _____

3. What is the perimeter (distance around) in feet of the entire field? _____

4. What is the area in feet of the actual NFL playing field from goal line to goal line? _____

5. What is total height of the goal post including the uprights? _____

6. What is the area of the rectangle formed by the uprights? _____

7. What is the area of one end zone? _____

8. What is the perimeter of one end zone? _____

9. What is the area of one sideline? _____

10. What is the total area of the NFL football field, including both sidelines and both end zones?

_____

Rushing Statistics

Directions: Use your math skills to do these problems based on the performance of NFL rushers. Circle the correct operation and compute the solution. (**Note:** The statistics and teams of current players were up-to-date at the time of publication of this book.)

1. Emmitt Smith of the Dallas Cowboys had 148 career touchdowns. Jerome Bettis of the Steelers had 53 career touchdowns. How many more touchdowns did Emmitt Smith have?

    Addition   Subtraction   Multiplication   Division   **Solution** _____

2. In a game against the Panthers, New Orleans' Ricky Williams rushed for 147 yards on 31 carries. What was his average yards per carry?

    Addition   Subtraction   Multiplication   Division   **Solution** _____

3. Garrison Hearst of the 49ers had 18 career touchdowns. Curtis Martin of the Jets had 64 career touchdowns. How many career touchdowns did they have in all?

    Addition   Subtraction   Multiplication   Division   **Solution** _____

4. In one game Eddie George of Tennessee rushed for 96 yards against Minnesota. Michael Bennett of Minnesota rushed for 113 yards against Tennessee. How many yards did they rush for altogether?

    Addition   Subtraction   Multiplication   Division   **Solution** _____

5. When Stephen Davis of the Redskins had 38 career touchdowns, Terry Allen had 35 more touchdowns than Davis. How many touchdowns did Allen have?

    Addition   Subtraction   Multiplication   Division   **Solution** _____

6. When LaDainian Tomlinson of the Chargers had 10 career touchdowns, Terrell Davis of the Broncos had 6 times as many career touchdowns. How many career touchdowns did Davis have?

    Addition   Subtraction   Multiplication   Division   **Solution** _____

7. Priest Holmes of Kansas City rushed for 150 yards on 20 carries in a game against Pittsburgh. What was his average yards per carry?

    Addition   Subtraction   Multiplication   Division   **Solution** _____

8. Anthony Thomas of the Bears rushed for 188 yards on 22 carries against the Bengals. What was his average yards per carry?

    Addition   Subtraction   Multiplication   Division   **Solution** _____

Computing Pass Completion Percentages

To compute pass completion percentage, divide the number of passes completed by the number of passes attempted. Pass completion percentages are calculated to two places and written as percents—like 25%. Follow the steps to find pass completion percentages.

Example

Joe Montana attempted 25 passes in one game. He completed 17 passes. What was his passing percentage?

1. *Divide.* $25\overline{)17}$

2. *Add a decimal point and three zeroes.*

$$
\begin{array}{r}
.680 \\
25\overline{)17.000} \\
-15\,0 \\
\hline
2\,00 \\
-2\,00 \\
\hline
0
\end{array}
$$

3. *Round to two places.* .68

4. *Multiply by 100.* .68 x 100 = 68%

Joe Montana's passing percentage is 68%.

Directions: Compute these pass completion percentages. (**Note:** This statistics and teams of current players were up-to-date at the time of publication of this book.)

1. In a game against the New England Patriots, Kurt Warner of the St. Louis Rams threw 30 complete passes in 42 attempts. What was his pass completion percentage? _____

2. Rich Gannon of the Oakland Raiders had 31 completed passes in 46 attempts against Kansas City. What was his pass completion percentage? _____

3. Brett Farve of the Green Bay Packers had 27 completed passes in 34 attempts against the Baltimore Ravens. What was his passing percentage? _____

4. Donovan McNabb of the Philadelphia Eagles had 32 completed passes in 48 attempts against the St. Louis Rams. What was his pass completion percentage? _____

5. Peyton Manning of the Indianapolis Colts had 22 completed passes in 34 attempts against the Patriots. What was his pass completion percentage? _____

6. Doug Flutie of the San Diego Chargers had 23 completions in 38 attempts against the Cowboys. What was his pass completion percentage? _____

7. In Super Bowl XXXII, John Elway of the Denver Broncos completed 12 of 22 passes against the Packers. What was his pass completion percentage? _____

Comparing Yardage

Directions: Use your math skills to solve these football problems.

1. In his 13-year career, Walter Payton rushed for 16,776 yards. Barry Sanders rushed for 15,269 yards in his career. How many more yards did Payton gain? _____

2. Marcus Allen rushed for 12,243 yards in his career. Jim Brown rushed for 12,312 yards. How many fewer yards did Allen have?

   _____

3. Dan Marino passed for 61,361 yards in his 17-year career. John Elway passed for 51,475 yards. How many more yards did Marino pass for? _____

4. Joe Montana passed for 40,551 yards in his career. Steve Young passed for 33,124 yards. How many yards did they pass for altogether?

   _____

5. In 16 years, Sammy Baugh punted for 15,245 yards. In 11 years, Tommy Davis punted for 22,833 yards. How many more yards did Davis punt for?

   _____

6. Gale Sayers gained 2,781 yards on kickoff returns. Travis Williams gained 2,801 yards on kickoff returns. How many fewer yards did Sayers gain? _____

7. In the year 2000, Brian Griese threw for 2,688 yards. Peyton Manning threw for 4,413 yards. How many yards did they throw for altogether? _____

8. In the 2000 football season, Doug Flutie threw for 1,700 yards. Elvis Grbac threw for 4,169 yards. How many more yards did Grbac throw for? _____

9. In the year 2000, Kurt Warner threw for 3,429 yards and Trent Green, on the same team, threw for 2,063 yards. How many yards did they pass for in all?

   _____

10. In the 2000 season, Torry Holt caught 82 passes for 1,635 yards. Marshall Faulk caught 81 passes for 830 yards. How many receiving yards did these two players get altogether? _____

Calculating Winning Percentages

You can calculate a team's winning percentage by dividing the number of games won by the number of games played. Winning percentages are calculated to three decimal places and written as a decimal—like batting averages. Follow the steps to calculate winning percentages.

Example

The New Orleans Saints won 10 of 16 games in the 2000 regular season.

1. *Divide.* $16\overline{)10}$

2. *Add a decimal and four zeroes.*

$$
\begin{array}{r}
.6250 \\
16\overline{)10.0000} \\
-9\,6 \\
\hline
40 \\
-32 \\
\hline
80 \\
-80 \\
\hline
0
\end{array}
$$

3. *Round the answer to three decimals.* 0.625

The New Orleans Saints' winning percentage is .625.

Directions: Compute the regular season winning percentages of these teams.

	Team	Won	Lost	Played	Winning Percentage
1.	Vikings	11	5	16	
2.	Jaguars	14	2	16	
3.	Dolphins	14	0	14	
4.	Colts	10	4	14	
5.	Cowboys	11	3	14	
6.	Packers	13	1	14	
7.	Vikings	15	1	16	
8.	Seahawks	9	7	16	
9.	Steelers	10	6	16	
10.	Browns	8	8	16	
11.	Bears	11	4	15	
12.	49ers	13	2	15	
13.	Raiders	12	4	16	
14.	Rams	13	3	16	
15.	Broncos	12	2	14	
16.	Titans	13	3	16	

1. Which team had the highest winning percentage? _____

2. Which team had a .500 winning percentage? _____

3. Which teams had identical winning percentages?_____

NFL Salaries

The graph below illustrates the growth in NFL salaries between 1970 and 1998.

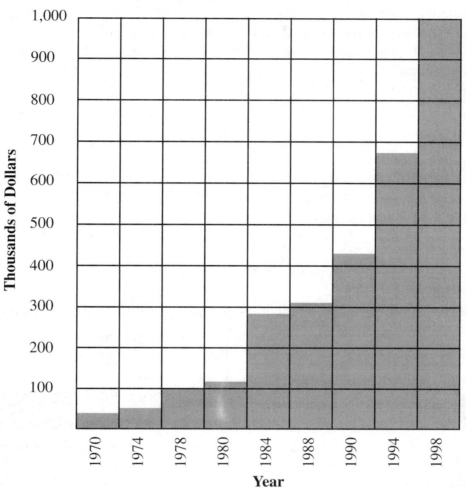

Directions: Study the bar graph above. Then answer these questions based on the graph.

1. In which year was the average NFL football salary about $40,000? _____
2. In which year did the average NFL salary become $1,000,000? _____
3. What is the difference between the average salary in 1978 and the average salary in 1998?

   _____

4. About how much was the average NFL salary in 1994? _____
5. In what year did the average salary become more than $300,000? _____
6. In what year did the average salary go over half a million dollars? _____
7. About how much was the average salary of NFL players in 1990? _____

Directions: Create a bar graph on graph paper comparing the number of years these running backs played in the NFL.

Jim Brown—9 years   Walter Payton—13 years

Marcus Allen—16 years   Barry Sanders—10 years

Franco Harris—13 years   Eric Dickerson—11 years

Herschel Walker—12 years   Jim Taylor—10 years

Football Chronology

Directions

1. Read the following chronology of some of the interesting events in football history.

2. Find at least 20 events in United States or world history that occurred on the dates listed below. **Examples:** The first transcontinental railroad was completed in 1869, the year the first football game was played. Franklin Roosevelt was elected President in 1932, the year of the first NFL championship game.

Helpful Hints

- Use encyclopedias, almanacs, football books, history texts, the Internet, and other sources.

- The events may include on-going wars, years a president was in office, and events such as the *Challenger* space shuttle crash.

- If you know of an important date in history, try to find other important events in football history that happened at the same time.

Football Chronology

1869 The first football game was played on Nov. 6 between Princeton and Rutgers Universities. The ball was round, like a soccer ball. There were 25 players on each team. A goal was worth 1 point. Rutgers won 6 to 4.

1869 In a rematch a week later, Princeton won 8 to 0. The custom of yelling and cheering by fans was initiated by Princeton students.

1870s Harvard developed its own game based on rugby. Players were allowed to pick up, catch, and run with the ball. The ball was egg-shaped and leather-covered.

1876 The Intercollegiate Football Association was formed by Ivy League colleges. A touchdown was worth 1 point. A field goal was worth 4 points.

1877 Teams were reduced to 15 players. A game was 90 minutes long.

1880s The father of modern football, Walter Camp of Yale University, convinced the Association to accept these basic concepts of modern football:

- continuous possession of the ball by one team for a series of three downs to gain 5 yards

- an organized scrimmage in which the quarterback took the snap and initiated play to replace a free-for-all rugby style

- marking the 5-yard lines which gave a gridiron look to the field

- teams had 11 players

1882 The first football uniform made of canvas. It was designed by L. P. Smock. Signals were used to call the plays. Blocking was introduced to protect the ball carrier.

Football Chronology *(cont.)*

1885 Touchdown points increased from 2 to 4. Points for a safety were raised to 2.

1890s Football games become a Thanksgiving tradition.

1894 University Athletic Club formed a rules committee with four Ivy League Colleges. Game length was shortened to two halves of 35 minutes each. A maximum of three players could be in motion before the snap.

1895 First professional game was played in Latrobe, Pennsylvania.

1902 The first professional league was formed by 3 Pennsylvania teams.

1905 The brutality of the game led to sweeping rule changes including:

1. no tackling out of bounds,
2. no piling on,
3. no hitting the ball carrier in the face,
4. 10 yards needed for first down,
5. game length was two halves of 30 minutes each,
6. the forward pass was legalized.

1908 Mass-formation plays were forbidden. Blockers could no longer lock arms against rushers. The flying tackle was banned. Crawling with the ball was prohibited.

1910 Game length was divided into four quarters of 15 minutes each.

The NCAA was founded to reform the game and make it safer.

1912 Teams were allowed four downs to make a first down. Field length was reduced to 100 yards. Touchdowns were worth 6 points.

1913 Notre Dame defeated Army with and popularized the forward pass.

1922 The National Football League was formed under the influence of George Halas who owned the Chicago Bears.

1925 Halas hired college star "Red" Grange, and 33,000 people came to watch his first game, the largest professional game—crowd at that time.

1926 The first college game to draw a 100,000-person crowd was played between Army and Navy.

1929 "Wrong Way" Riegel ran a recovered fumble 64 yards in the wrong direction in the Rose Bowl.

1932 The first NFL championship game was won by the Chicago Bears over the Green Bay Packers in a converted hockey stadium.

1937 All players were required to have numbers on their jerseys.

1939 The first televised football game was between the Brooklyn Dodgers football team and the Philadelphia Eagles. NCAA mandates wearing helmets.

1960 The American Football League was formed to compete with the NFL.

1961 The University of Maryland became the first team to put names on the back of players' jerseys.

1967 The Green Bay Packers won the first Super Bowl by defeating the Kansas City Chiefs 35–10.

1969 Joe Namath led the New York Jets to a sensational victory over the highly favored Baltimore Colts. The Super Bowl became a national sporting event.

1970 The AFL and NFL merged. The first Monday Night Football Game was telecast.

1972 The only undefeated season in NFL history was posted by the Miami Dolphins.

Where the Pros Play

Below is a list of the 32 NFL teams.

Directions: Label each team on the United States map on the next page. Then answer the questions on the bottom of the page. Please note that the information here was correct at the time of this book's publication. Sometimes teams change locations.

NFL Teams

Arizona Cardinals	Green Bay Packers	Oakland Raiders
Atlanta Falcons	Houston Texans	Philadelphia Eagles
Baltimore Ravens	Indianapolis Colts	Pittsburgh Steelers
Buffalo Bills	Jacksonville Jaguars	San Diego Chargers
Carolina Panthers	Kansas City Chiefs	San Francisco Forty Niners
Chicago Bears	Miami Dolphins	Seattle Seahawks
Cincinnati Bengals	Minnesota Vikings	St. Louis Rams
Cleveland Browns	New England Patriots	Tampa Bay Buccaneers
Dallas Cowboys	New Orleans Saints	Tennessee Titans
Denver Broncos	New York Giants	Washington Redskins
Detroit Lions	New York Jets	

NFL Questions

1. How many states have an NFL team? _____

2. How many NFL teams play in California? _____

3. How many NFL teams are located in cities west of the Mississippi River? _____

4. How many NFL teams are located in cities east of the Mississippi River? _____

5. Which state have the most NFL teams? _____

6. How many states have no NFL teams? _____

7. How many NFL teams play in Florida? _____

8. How many NFL teams play in Pennsylvania? _____

60

United States Map

Directions: Use this map to complete **Where the Pros Play** (page 60) and **The College Game** (page 63).

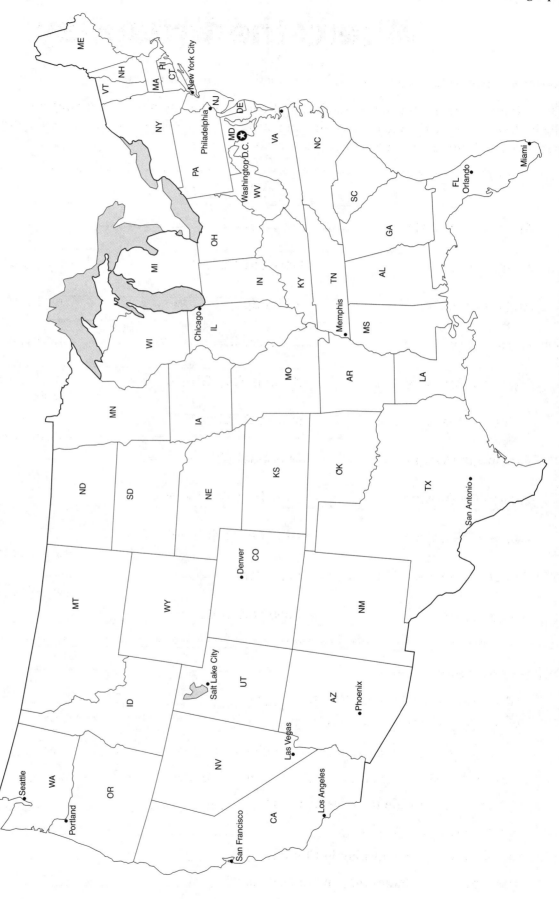

What's in a Name?

Directions: Use a dictionary and your imagination to suggest the meaning of each team's name. Write why you think each club chose its name.

Bears _____

Bengals _____

Bills _____

Broncos _____

Browns _____

Buccaneers _____

Cardinals _____

Chargers _____

Chiefs _____

Colts _____

Cowboys _____

Dolphins _____

Eagles _____

Falcons _____

49ers _____

Giants _____

Jaguars _____

Jets _____

Lions _____

Packers _____

Panthers _____

Patriots _____

Raiders _____

Rams _____

Ravens _____

Redskins _____

Seahawks _____

Steelers _____

Texans _____

Titans _____

Vikings _____

1. Which teams are named after birds? _____

2. Which teams are named after mammals? _____

62

The College Game

Football is an immensely popular game on American college campuses, and colleges have created some colorful names for the teams that represent them.

Directions: Listed below are some of the great college and university teams in the United States. Write each college in the correct state on the map on page 61. Then see how many of the nicknames you can match to each one.

College/University	Location (city/state)	Nicknames
Arkansas	Fayetteville, AR	Badgers
Alabama	Tuscaloosa, AL	Bruins
Boston College	Chestnut Hill, MA	Terrapins
Florida	Gainesville, FL	Midshipman
Florida State	Tallahassee, FL	Trojans
Georgia Tech	Atlanta, GA	Yellow Jackets
Grambling	Grambling, LA	Cardinal
Illinois	Urbana, IL	Cornhuskers
Maryland	College Park, MD	Ducks
Miami	Coral Gables, FL	Red Raiders
Michigan	Ann Arbor, MI	Crimson Tide
Michigan State	East Lansing, MI	Gators
Navy	Annapolis, MD	Hurricanes
Nebraska	Lincoln, NE	Volunteers
Notre Dame	Notre Dame, IN	Tigers
Oklahoma	Norman, OK	Fighting Irish
Ohio State	Columbus, OH	Spartans
Oregon	Eugene, OR	Nittany Lions
Penn State	University Park, PA	Boilermakers
Purdue	West Lafayette, IN	Eagles
Stanford	Stanford, CA	Seminoles
Tennessee	Knoxville, TN	Wolverines
Texas Tech	Lubbock, TX	Razorbacks
UCLA	Los Angeles, CA	Fighting Illini
USC	Los Angeles, CA	Sooners
Wisconsin	Madison, WI	Mountaineers
West Virginia	Morgantown, WV	Buckeyes

Sports Around the World

American football is most popular in the United States, although it is also played in Europe. Every country has games and sports that are enjoyed by their citizens.

Directions: Use atlases, encyclopedias, almanacs, the Internet, and other sources to complete the following activities.

1. Label each of these countries on the world map (page 65). If the country is very small, draw an arrow with the name of the country.
2. Next to the countries listed below, name one popular sport or game in that country.
3. Add five countries of your own and repeat the steps above.

Country	**Sport/Game**
1. England	_____
2. Canada	_____
3. Mexico	_____
4. Japan	_____
5. Germany	_____
6. France	_____
7. Brazil	_____
8. China	_____
9. South Korea	_____
10. Spain	_____
11. South Africa	_____
12. Thailand	_____
13. Philippines	_____
14. Switzerland	_____
15. Norway	_____
16. Ireland	_____
17. Chile	_____
18. Italy	_____
19. Australia	_____
20. Venezuela	_____
21. Argentina	_____
22. Sweden	_____
23. Israel	_____
24. Romania	_____
25. Kenya	_____
26. _____	_____
27. _____	_____
28. _____	_____
29. _____	_____
30. _____	_____

Which sports or games seem to be popular in many countries? _____

World Map

Directions: Use this map with **Sports Around the World** (page 64).

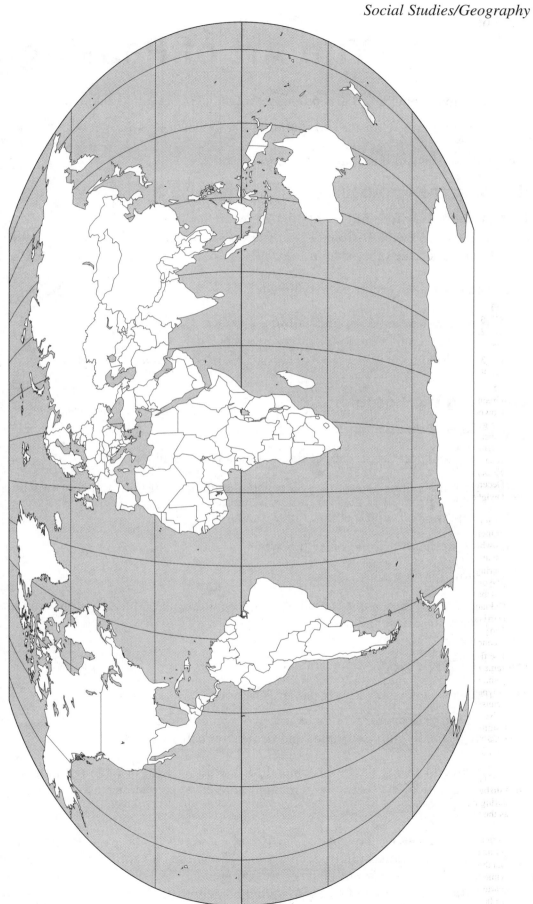

The Art of Passing

- A football spins when it is properly thrown. This is called a spiral.
- A football travels faster and more accurately when it is thrown with a spiral.

Follow these steps to throw a perfect spiral.

Gripping the Football

1. Place three or four fingers of your throwing hand over the laces of the ball. Spread your fingers so that the thumb is on the other side of the ball.

2. The laces help you grip the ball better.

3. You do not have to grip the ball in the center. Your grip may be predominantly to the back of the ball.

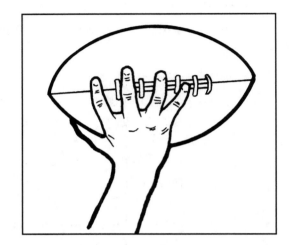

Throwing the Football

1. Hold your arm a little above your ear.

2. Keep your feet apart—about the width of your shoulders.

3. Point your opposite foot (if you're righthanded, point your left foot) towards your target.

4. Throw the ball with a sharp, quick snap.

5. Look in the direction you're throwing.

6. Follow through with your arm motion.

7. If a receiver is moving, anticipate his direction and lead him by throwing ahead of where he is when you release the ball.

Passing Practice

The only way to become a good passer is to practice.

- Practice with smaller footballs until you get comfortable with the motion. Use soft, foam balls and gradually move to larger and firmer footballs.

- Practice throwing the ball back and forth with a friend or a family member. Start out with short passes only a few feet long. Gradually increase the distance as you improve your technique and your accuracy.

- Practice throwing the ball at a surface of some type. Make a mark on a garage wall, a baseball backstop, a tennis wall, or even a tree. Throw the ball softly at first from short distances. Gradually increase your distance as you practice. Adjust your grip on the ball until you find one that fits your hand and gives you good ball control.

Kicking the Ball

Michelle was a successful kicker when she used good technique and focused on her objectives. Follow these suggestions to improve your kicking success.

The Kickoff

The kickoff is used to start a game; to begin the second half of a game; and after a touchdown or field goal scored.

To kick the ball:

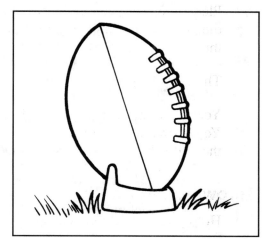

1. Place the ball on the kicking tee with the laces facing away from you.
2. Stand about 7 to 10 steps behind the ball.
3. Run with an even stride toward the ball.
4. Land so that the kicking foot is directly behind the ball.
5. Keep your head down and your eyes on the ball.
6. Kick just below the center of the ball.
7. Follow through by lifting the kicking foot and bending forward.

Kicking the Point After Touchdown (PAT)

The ball is placed on the 2-yard line in front of the goal posts. The center snaps the ball to the holder. The holder places one end of the ball on the ground with the laces facing away from the kicker and holds the ball upright from the other end with 2 fingers.

To kick the ball:

1. Stand two steps behind the ball, feet a few inches apart, weight evenly balanced, knees slightly bent, arms loose, body bent slightly forward, and kicking toe pointed at the ball.
2. Step off with the kicking foot.
3. Take the second step with the opposite foot.
4. Keep your head down and your eyes on the ball.
5. Kick at or just below the center of the ball.
6. Follow through by lifting the kicking foot and bending forward.

Kicking Field Goals

A field goal can be attempted from any place on the field. The technique is the same used for kicking the point after touchdown.

Kicking the Ball *(cont.)*

Punting the Ball

The punt is one of the most difficult kicks in football.

Follow these steps to improve your punting.

1. Stand relaxed, a few feet behind the center with your kicking foot a few inches ahead of the other foot.

2. Bend your knees and lean forward as the ball is snapped.

3. Hold your hands open and relaxed at knee level to catch the snap.

4. Lift the ball so that it is waist high and parallel to the ground.

5. Rotate the ball so that the laces face up and away from the foot.

6. Take one short step with your kicking foot.

7. Take one long step with your non-kicking foot.

8. Swing the kicking foot forward, lock your ankle, and release the ball about a foot above the ground.

9. Your instep (not your toe) should stride into the ball.

10. Follow through by straightening your knee and lifting your leg.

11. Keep your eye on the ball and support your weight on the other foot.

12. Practice so that your punts spiral just like good passes.

Checking the Text

Elaine Moore carefully describes how Michelle kicks the ball when she makes a place kick or a kickoff.

Directions: Find a passage in the book, *Get That Girl Out of the Boy's Locker Room!*, such as on page 28 that describes Michelle's kicking style. Describe step by step Michelle's technique for a place kick or kickoff.

Page _____

Description

1. _____

2. _____

3. _____

4. _____

5. _____

6. _____

Exercise

You will play better football and be healthier in general if you exercise sensibly, eat wisely, and get regular sleep every night.

Exercise Tips

- Get 20 to 30 minutes of exercise at least five days a week.

- Start at a relaxed pace and then speed up when you are warmed up.

- Do stretching exercises, practice calisthenics, jump rope, and do other similar activities for coordination.

- Run for a few minutes. Start out rather slowly and gradually increase the pace.

- Divide your exercise period into brief, 10-minute chunks and use these exercise periods as breaks from studying. They will help you concentrate better when you return to your studies.

- Substitute 30 minutes of exercise for television viewing, video-game playing, or other sedentary activities.

- Practice passing and catching the football with anyone who will practice with you. It doesn't matter if they are younger or older. You can learn from the more experienced players and help less-skilled players.

- Balance football with other sports that require lots of physical activity such as soccer, bicycling, and basketball.

- Keep a weekly exercise and study log like the one below to help you balance your activities and use your time well.

Exercise and Study Log

Date _____

Time(s)_____

Type of Exercise _____

Study Time(s)_____

Measuring Your Pulse Rate

1. Find your pulse on the underside of your wrist or at the carotid artery on your neck.

2. Place the index and middle finger on your wrist and count the number of beats for one minute.

   Resting Pulse Rate _____

3. Exercise for 10 to 15 minutes by jumping rope, walking fast, running, or doing some other moderately vigorous exercise.

4. Take your pulse again.

   Pulse Rate After Exercise _____

Nutrition

"You are what you eat."

For athletes and non-athletes, it is very important to eat a balanced diet, rich in nutrients, especially as your body is going through a time of rapid change. The food pyramid shown here illustrates the need to maintain a diet heavy in carbohydrates, fruits, and vegetables.

Food Pyramid

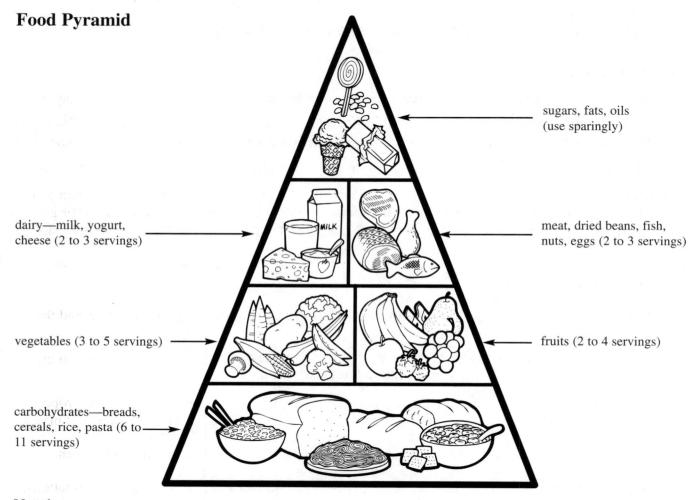

sugars, fats, oils (use sparingly)

dairy—milk, yogurt, cheese (2 to 3 servings)

meat, dried beans, fish, nuts, eggs (2 to 3 servings)

vegetables (3 to 5 servings)

fruits (2 to 4 servings)

carbohydrates—breads, cereals, rice, pasta (6 to 11 servings)

Nutrients

- *Carbohydrates* provide the body with energy.
- *Vitamins* help the body grow and repair itself and prevent illness.
- *Minerals* aid in growth and repair.
- *Protein* is essential for building the body and repair.
- *Fats* supply concentrated energy and help form hormones, which are chemical messengers in the body.

Daily Nutrition Record

Directions: Keep a record of what you eat for one 24-hour period. Include what you eat for breakfast, lunch, dinner, and snacks. Compare what you ate to the food pyramid above. How close did you come to the recommended daily servings?

Football at School

Tackle football is never allowed at any school except by a team in full uniform with a coach and all appropriate safety equipment. Two forms of intramural football are played at many elementary and middle schools: touch football and flag football.

There are two basic rules common to both sports:

1. A player may never tackle.
2. A player may never block another player with his feet off the ground.

Touch Football/Flag Football

The rules are very flexible and may vary according to many conditions such as the size of the playing field, time constraints, and the number of children who wish to play. These are the general rules:

- **Time:** Four quarters of 5 to 10 minutes each. The longer time might be used in a P.E. period. At recess, the length of the game could be the length of the recess.

- **Playing Field:** Most schools do not have a field with 100 yards, marked yard lines, or even goal posts. Use red plastic warning cones or some other material to indicate the end zone and/or goal posts.

- **Touch, Don't Tackle:** Do not tackle a player ever. Agree on the rules—one-hand touch, two-hand touch, or flag football—before the game begins.

  1. In *one-hand touch football*, a player must touch the ball carrier between the shoulder and the knees with only one hand.

  2. In *two-hand touch football*, a player must touch the ball carrier between the shoulder and the knees with both hands at the same time.

  3. In *flag football*, every player wears a piece of cloth or "flag" in his belt or tucked on a rope that is tied around the waist. The opposing player grabs the flag instead of touching the player.

- **Stopping the Play:** The play stops where the ball carrier was touched or the flag was taken.

- **Number of Players:** You may play with a full 11 players on each team using regular formations. With fewer players, try to have at least three or four players on the line with fewer players in the backfield.

- **The Kickoff:** A team may use a regular kickoff or punt the ball to begin a game or to resume the game after a touchdown.

- **Blocking:** Only the shoulders, chest, and arms may be used in blocking. Body blocks, flying or leaping blocks, blocks below the knees or above the shoulders are not allowed. An automatic first down is awarded to any team that is the victim of an illegal block.

Football at School *(cont.)*

- **First Down:** On larger and longer fields, a team may receive a first down by advancing the ball 20 yards or more with its four downs. On shorter fields, a team may only get the four downs to score with the football. The 4th down may be used to try to score or to kick the ball deep into the opponent's territory.

- **Scoring:** Scoring is usually limited to touchdowns, although teams may kick, run, or pass for points after a touchdown if both teams agree. A field goal can be used if both teams agree.

- **Fumbles:** Play stops immediately when a ball is fumbled. The team that had the ball keeps it.

- **Passing:** The quarterback must make a forward pass only from behind the line of scrimmage. Lateral passes (a pass to a player alongside the passer) may be made at any time.

- **The Count:** Some touch football games require an audible three count from a defensive player (one, one thousand; two, one thousand; three, one thousand) after the snap before the defensive players may rush the quarterback. This allows for a more exciting game. Agree on this rule before the game begins.

- **Violations:** The following violations are usually enforced:

  1. A team loses the ball if an illegal block is used.

  2. An illegal tackle results in an automatic first down for the team with the ball.

  3. A player exhibiting poor sportsmanship is removed from the game.

Set the Rules

Review the rules listed above. Team captains and some team members should agree on all rules to be followed in your game. List the agreed upon rules below.

Time: _____

Playing Field: _____

One-hand touch, two-hand touch, or flag: _____

Number of players: _____

Scoring: _____

First down: _____

The count: _____

Violations and punishments: _____

Logos and Posters

Imagine that you have created your own football team in a new league. It might be a league just for children, a girls' league, or a flag football team.

Logos

Directions: In the circles below, design several logos for your team and other teams in the league. Be dramatic. Make them colorful. Create unusual designs.

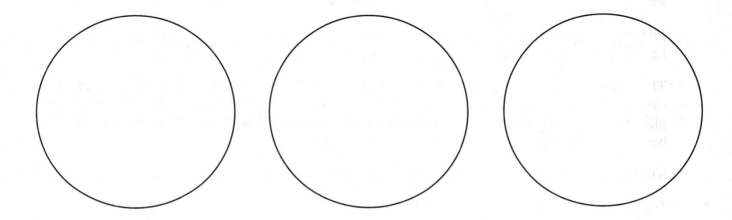

Posters

Directions: Create a football poster design for your team in the rectangles below. Use these designs to make full-size posters on large construction paper.

Design Your Own Football Uniform

Imagine that you have been asked to design a new uniform for a football team. It might be a league just for children, a girls' league, or a flag football team.

Directions: Create your own design for a team uniform. Keep in mind the following when designing the uniform.

- Choose the colors to be worn.

- Decide where you want to place the name of the team, the name of the player, and the player's number.

- If you designed a logo (page 73), you will probably want to use that in your design.

- Consider entirely different options: Use a separate sheet of paper to design a completely different style of helmet, pads in different places, and totally different styles of jerseys and pants.

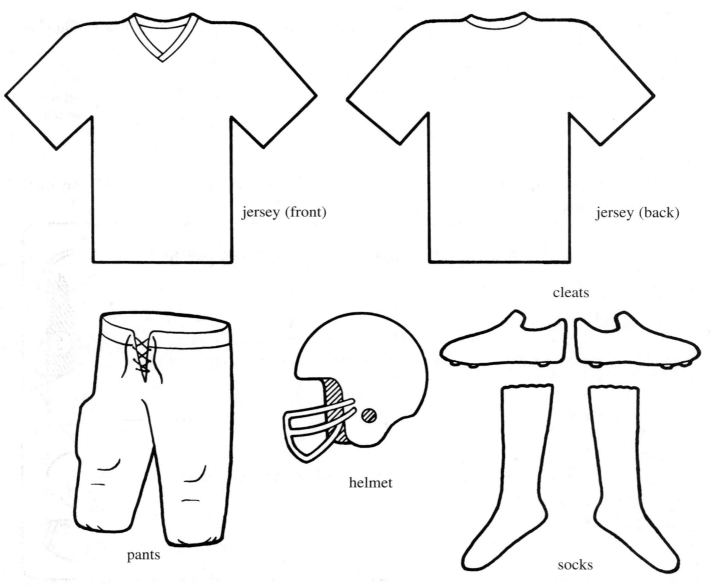

jersey (front)

jersey (back)

cleats

pants

helmet

socks

Super Bowl

The Super Bowl is the biggest football game of the year. It is the game played for the NFL championship.

Declare a specific day as Super Bowl Friday. (Any day will work, but Friday is a day kids can anticipate all week.)

1. Each student in the class could come dressed in a football uniform. Encourage students to borrow from friends or to look through closets for useful items.

2. Divide your class into two teams of equal ability. Each team should have an equal number of players. Each team will start 11 players, if you wish, but be sure that all children get an opportunity to play. (Student leaders often create very good teams, if you provide direction.)

3. Set aside a long afternoon period for a flag or touch football game between the two teams.

4. Review the rules for flag or touch football with the students. See Football at School on pages 71 and 72.

5. Select timekeepers and scorekeepers from among students who are unable to play due to injury or special needs.

6. Try to get a parent or high-school student to officiate the game.

7. In keeping with the football theme of the day, consider a luncheon with a football motif and some of the students' favorite stadium foods (hot dogs, chips, etc.). Enlist several parents to help with the cooking and organization of the luncheon.

8. Award Super Bowl Certificates (page 78) to all students who participate.

9. Take pictures and create a bulletin board display of this activity entitled: Super Bowl Friday from Room _____.

Super Bowl Day is Here!

Dear _____,

   We are planning a day of celebration as we complete our football unit. Can you help us prepare our luncheon? Please fill out the information below and return it by _____.

I can prepare the following food: _____

_____

I can donate the following items (paper goods, drinks, etc.):

_____

Parent Name: _____   Phone #: _____

Bulletin Board Ideas

Super Bowl Highlights

Take pictures at your Super Bowl game day and display them, possibly mixed in with a collage of action shots of NFL players. Be sure to include the luncheon and other activities from that day (page 75).

Football Poems and Other Spirals

Display Pigskin Poetry (page 43) on construction paper footballs. Make some mini-footballs made with cups and tennis balls. Mount these on the board to provide a three-dimensional effect.

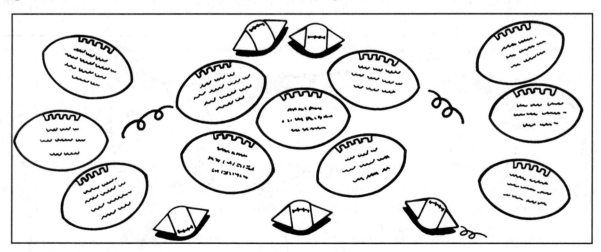

Additional Ideas

- *Highlight the Books*—Encourage students to choose their favorite scenes from *Get That Girl Out of the Boys' Locker Room!* and *Catch That Pass!*. Ask students to illustrate these scenes with simple line drawings, colored pencils, markers, or any other available media. Post this student artwork.

- *Football Signals*—Create a display showing various football signals highlighted in the book (page 17).

Bulletin Board Ideas *(cont.)*

Football Word Wall

Create a bulletin board that looks like a football field. Use some of the words and phrases highlighted in **Football Terms**, **Football Lingo**, and **Where the Action Is** (pages 46 through 48). Have students draw pictures to illustrate the words.

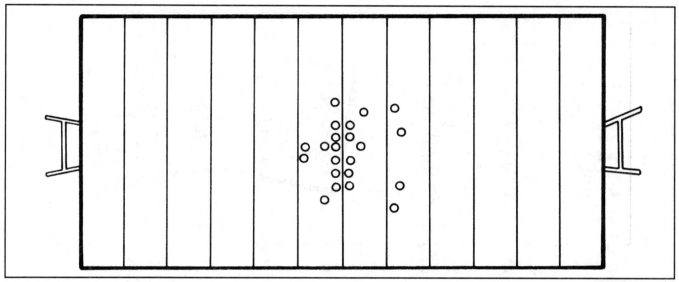

Where the Pros Play

Post a large map of the United States. Ask students to locate each NFL city (page 60) on the map with a flag or symbol of the team. Use the same map to locate the college teams mentioned in **The College Game** (page 63).

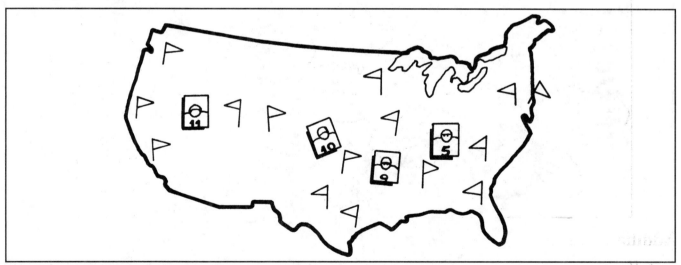

Additional Ideas

- *Heroes of the Game*—Ask students to draw pictures of the famous football player they researched (pages 32 and 33). Post the pictures and their reports.

- *Logos and Posters*—Create a display of the logos and posters that the students have designed (page 73).

Super Bowl Certificate

Super Bowl Award

"It's All Teamwork"

This award is presented to

in recognition of exceptional

Team Spirit ★ Leadership ★ Initiative

Signed

Date

Bibliography

Fiction

- **Other books by Matt Christopher (published by Little, Brown)**

  Basketball Sparkplug, 1957.
  Center Court Sting, 1998.
  Football Fugitive, 1988.
  Football Nightmare, 2001.
  Long Arm Quarterback, 1999.

  Soccer Halfback, 1985.
  The Basket Counts, 1991.
  The Catcher with a Glass Arm, 1985.
  The Hockey Machine, 1986.

- ***The Trick* series by Scott Corbett (published by Little, Brown)**

  The Baseball Trick, 1965.
  The Disappearing Dog Trick, 1963.
  The Hairy Horror Trick, 1969.
  The Hangman's Ghost Trick, 1977

  The Hockey Trick, 1974.
  The Home Run Trick, 1973.
  The Lemonade Trick, 1960.
  The Mailbox Trick, 1961.

- ***The Great Brain* series by John D. Fitzgerald (published by Dial)**

  More Adventures of the Great Brain, 1969.
  The Great Brain, 1967.
  The Great Brain at the Academy, 1972.

  The Great Brain Does It Again, 1975
  The Great Brain Reforms, 1975
  The Return of the Great Brain, 1974.

- **Other books by Elaine Moore**

  Chocolate Daze (Troll, 1997)
  Grandma's Garden (Lothrop, 1994)
  Grandma's House (Lothrop, 1985)
  Grandma's Promise (Lothrop, 1988)

  Grandma's Smile (Lothrop, 1995)
  I'd Rather Be Eaten by Sharks (Scholastic, 1995)
  The Substitute Teacher from Mars (Troll, 1993)
  Who Let Girls in the Boys' Locker Room?
  (Troll, 1996)

- ***The Soup* series by Robert Newton Peck (published by Knopf)**

  Soup, 1974.
  Soup & Me, 1975
  Soup for President, 1998.
  Soup in the Saddle, 1983.
  Soup on Ice, 1985.

  Soup on Wheels, 1981.
  Soup's Drum, 1980.
  Soup's Goat, 1984.
  Soup 1776, 1995.
  Soup Ahoy, 1994.

Non-fiction

Creighton, Jayne. *Boomerangs, Blades & Basketballs: The Science of Sports.* (Science and Work Series) Raintree, Steck-Vaughn Publishers, 2000.

Christopher, Matt. *On the Court with . . . Michael Jordan.* Little, Brown, 1996.

Poetry

Hall, Donald (ed.). *The Oxford Illustrated Book of American Children's Poems.* Oxford University Press, 2001.

Hopkins, Lee Bennett. *Opening Days: Sports Poems.* Harcourt Children's Books, 1996.

Panzer, Nora (ed.). *Celebrate America in Poetry and Art.* Hyperion Books for Children, 1994.

Internet Web Sites

http://www.elainemoore.com
http://www.womensprofootball.com

http://www.wafff.com
http://www.football.com

Answer Key

Page 20
1. C 3. C 5. B 7. C 9. D
2. B 4. A 6. A 8. B 10. B

Page 27
1. D 3. C 5. B 7. B 9. A
2. A 4. C 6. C 8. B 10. B

Page 28
1. Green Bay Packers vs. Dallas Cowboys. The Packers won the game 21–17 and a third consecutive NFL title; Bart Starr's last-minute, 1-yard sneak won the game in 13-below temperatures on December 31, 1967.
2. Dwight Clark caught a pass from Joe Montana during the final minutes of the San Francisco 49ers vs. Dallas Cowboys 1982 NFC Championship game.
3. During a 1972 divisional playoff game between the Pittsburgh Steelers vs. Oakland Raiders, Franco Harris caught a pass from Terry Bradshaw during the last seconds of the game.
4. The first televised football game was in 1939. It was a game between Fordham and Waynesburg College of Pennsylvania. It was played in New York City and Fordham won 34–7.
5. Dick Lane was a cornerback who was known as "Night Train" during his football playing days.
6. Pittsburgh Steelers defense during the 1970s was known as the "Steel Curtain."
7. a college player who participates in practices but is not active for games
8. members of the 1922 Notre Dame football team: quarterback Harry Stuhldreher, left halfback Jim Crowley, right halfback Don Miller, and fullback Elmer Layden; named after mythical lore of the Four Horsemen of the Apocalypse: famine, pestilence, destruction, and death
9. defensive tackle/fullback for the 1985 Super Bowl champion Chicago Bears
10. a deep, high throw by a quarterback down the field to a group of wide receivers and/or other players in the hopes that it will be caught

Pages 29 and 30
Joe Montana
College: Notre Dame
College statistics: 268 completions; 515 attempts; 25 touchdowns
Length of time in NFL: 15 years

Teams played for: San Francisco 49ers, Kansas City Chiefs
Passes attempted: 4,149
Complete passes: 2,667
Total passing yards: 40,551
Touchdowns: 273
Interceptions: 139
Average yards per attempted pass: 9.8 yards
NFL quarterback rating points: 92.3
Playoff appearances: 11 playoff appearances; 9 divisional championships
Super Bowl appearances: 4
Career Highlights, Influence on the Game, and Personal Characteristics: Answers may vary.

Steve Young
College: Brigham Young University
College statistics: 306 completions; 439 attempts; 33 touchdowns
Length of time in NFL: 15 years
Teams played for: Tampa Bay Buccaneers, San Francisco 49ers
Passes attempted: 4,149
Completed passes: 2,667
Total passing yards: 33,124
Touchdowns: 232
Interceptions: 107
Average yards per attempted pass: 8 yards
NFL quarterback rating points: 96.8
Playoff appearances: 7
Super Bowl appearances: 1
Career Highlights, Influence on the Game, and Personal Characteristics: Answers may vary

Dan Marino
College: University of Pittsburgh
College statistics: 625 completions; 1,085 attempts; 74 touchdowns
Length of time in the NFL: 17 years
Teams played for: Miami Dolphins
Passes attempted: 8,358
Completed passes: 4,967
Total passing yards: 61,361
Touchdowns: 420
Interceptions: 252
Average yards per attempted pass: 7.3 yards
NFL quarterback rating points: 86.4
Playoff appearances: 7
Super Bowl appearance: 1
Career Highlights, Influence on the Game, and Personal Characteristics: Answers may vary.

Page 31
Walter Payton
College: Jackson State University
College statistics: 4,037 yards
Length of time in NFL: 13 years
Teams played for: Chicago Bears
Rushing attempts: 3,838
Rushing yards: 16,726
Average yards per attempted rush: 4.4 yards
Touchdowns: 110

Total yards: 21,264
Longest run: 76 yards
Playoff appearances: 4
Super Bowl appearance: 1
Career Highlights and Personal Characteristics: Answers may vary.

Emmitt Smith
College: Florida State
College statistics: 3,928 yards
Length of time in the NFL: 11 years
Teams played for: Dallas Cowboys
Rushing attempts: 3,537
Rushing yards: 15,166
Average yards per attempted rush: 4.3 yards
Touchdowns: 145
Total yards: 17,973 yards
Longest run: 75
Playoff appearances: 7
Super Bowl appearances: 3
Career Highlights and Personal Characteristics: Answers may vary.

Page 48
intercepted intercepting
sacked
passing
rushed rushing
kicked kicking
squirted squirting
smashed smashing
blitzed blitzing
crushed crushing
launched launching
unloaded unloading
smashed smashing
spiked spiking
tackled tackling
fumbled fumbling
huddled huddling
exploded exploding
slammed slamming
driving
sweeping

Page 49
1. spiked   6. clipped
2. kicked   7. blitzing
3. blocking   8. faked
4. passing   9. tackling
5. sacked   10. encroaching

Page 50
1. pigskin
2. kickoff
3. delay of game
4. wide receiver, tightend, fullback, halfback
5. uprights, goalpost
6. hand off
7. suicide squad
8. first down
9. coin toss
10. piling on

Page 52
1. 300 ft.   7. 3,000 sq. ft.
2. 360 ft.   8. 260 ft.
3. 980 ft.   9. 1,000 sq. yd.
4. 30,000 sq. ft.   (not counting
5. 40 sq. ft.   the end zone)
6. 555 sq. ft.   10. 57,000 sq. ft.

Page 53
1. subtraction; 95 touchdowns
2. division; 4.7 yds.
3. addition; 82 touchdowns
4. addition; 209 yds.
5. addition; 73 touchdowns
6. multiplication; 60 touchdowns
7. division; 7.5 yds.
8. division; 8.5 yds.

Page 54
1. 71%   4. 67%   6. 61%
2. 67%   5. 65%   7. 55%
3. 79%

Page 55
1. 1,507 yds.   6. 20 yds.
2. 69 yds.   7. 7,101 yds.
3. 9,886 yds.   8. 2,469 yds.
4. 73,675 yds.   9. 5,492 yds.
5. 7,588 yds.   10. 2,465 yds.

Page 56
1. .688   7. .938   12. .867
2. .875   8. .563   13. .750
3. 1.000   9. .625   14. .813
4. .714   10. .500   15. .857
5. .786   11. .733   16. .813
6. .929

1. Dolphins   3. Rams; Titans
2. Browns

Page 57
1. 1970   5. 1988
2. 1998   6. 1988
3. $900,000   7. $440,000
4. $680,000

Page 60
1. 22 states and Washington, D.C.
2. 3
3. 12
4. 20
5. New York, California, and Florida have three each.
6. 28 states
7. 3
8. 2

Page 63
College/University
Arkansas Razorbacks
Alabama Crimson Tide
Boston College Eagles
Florida Gators
Florida State Seminoles
Georgia Tech Yellow Jackets
Grambling Tigers
Illinois Fighting Illini
Maryland Terrapins
Miami Hurricanes
Michigan Wolverines
Michigan State Spartans
Navy Midshipmen
Nebraska Cornhuskers
Notre Dame Fighting Irish
Oklahoma Sooners
Ohio State Buckeyes
Oregon Ducks
Penn State Nittany Lions
Purdue Boilermakers
Stanford Cardinal
Tennessee Volunteers
Texas Tech Red Raiders
UCLA Bruins